DIESTERWEGS
NEUSPRACHLICHE
BIBLIOTHEK

Short Stories of the Australian Experience

edited by
Thomas Rau

DIESTERWEG

Druck A² / Jahr 2011
Alle Drucke der Serie A sind im Unterricht parallel verwendbar.

Redaktion: Angela Wesser, Stuttgart
Umschlagfoto: Julia Gebhardt / pixelio.de
Umschlagkonzeption: Blum-Design und Kommunikation, Hamburg
Herstellung und Umschlagrealisation: Harald Thumser, Frankfurt
Satz: Stahringer Satz GmbH, Grünberg
Druck und Bindung: pva, Druck und Medien-Dienstleistungen GmbH, Landau

ISBN 978-3-425-**04825**-3

Table of Contents

Introduction

Each of the five stories is a reflection of the *Zeitgeist* of Australia at the time of its publication and deals with aspects of Australia considered relevant at the time. Being well-crafted and of exceptional literary worth, the short stories still appeal to the reader today because of the insights they provide about the Australian "soul" and because of the universality of their themes. It is also important to bear in mind that these short stories are embedded[1] within the unique parameters[2] of Australia's past and present.

What are these parameters? Australia is a relatively young, predominantly English-speaking immigrant society planted on a continent that had been the site of a widely-scattered civilisation, estimated to have been established 40,000 to 50,000 years ago. The tension between the pre-historic civilisation of the first dwellers of this continent, the Aborigines, and that of the British Europeans, who first reached its shores towards the end of the 18th century, is frequently evident in Australian literature (one unpleasant side effect of this tension being racism). The fact that Australia, for the first three quarters of the 19th century, was used to transport convicts[3] from Great Britain, often thrown into prison for the most trivial reasons, has also left an indelible[4] mark on the Australian psyche[5] and its literature. Furthermore, the convict experience encouraged anti-British sentiments and a contempt[6] for authority. Finally, Australia is slowly moving away from its European influence and increasingly embracing[7] Asia in terms of immigration, trade, and culture.

Each of these short stories portrays an aspect of Australia that is by its very nature as a literary work limited by the subjective perspective of the author. It is up to the reader in his or her critical assessment[8] of these short stories to compensate for and make corrective adjustments for any perceived[9] shortcomings.

---

1 to be embedded: to be firmly fixed in s.th.
2 parameter [pə'ræmɪtəʳ]: any constant or limiting factor
3 convict: a person found guilty of a crime and sent to prison
4 indelible [ɪn'deləbl]: permanent
5 psyche [saɪki]: deepest feelings and attitude
6 contempt: complete disrespect for s.th. or s.o.
7 to embrace (formal): to accept s.th. with enthusiasm
8 assessment: judgement or opinion of s.th. or s.o. after careful thought
9 to perceive: to notice

The first two stories have as their time frame the end of the 19th or beginning of the 20th century. *How Muster-Master Stoneman Earned His Breakfast*, condemns in no uncertain terms the penal[10] experiment of the 19th century as inhumane, sadistic, and counterproductive. It might be argued that the portrayal of this system is too simplistic. Anti-authoritarian and anti-British feelings are plain[11] to see.

The Drover's Wife exposes[12] the harshness[13], loneliness, and dangers of life in the outback. The author provides the female protagonist with heroic proportions, whereas the Aborigines play a subordinate[14] role. In *Marlene* the supercilious[15] and patronising[16] attitude of a member of the ruling classes towards Aborigines is brought to light.

The last two short stories *Coming Home* and *Neighbours* reflect a more recent Australia.
Coming Home is rather straightforward in its delineation[17] of racism and the inner identity conflict of a football hero of mixed blood. *Neighbours* is deceptive[18] in its simplicity: here lies much below the surface of a story of reversed roles. It is the young couple of old European stock[19], reminiscent of the hippie movement of the 1960s in America, who discover their common humanity with their neighbours, recently arrived immigrants.

The knowledge and insights acquired from these short stories can serve to deepen an understanding of Australia and its literature and indeed can find application in other contexts.

What parallels can you find to the literature and history of North America?

---

10 penal [ˈpiːnəl]: having to do with punishment by law
11 plain [pleɪn]: clear
12 to expose: to show, to reveal
13 harshness: difficult and unpleasant quality
14 subordinate [səˈbɔːdənət]: of less importance
15 supercilious [ˌsuːpəˈsɪliəs]: arrogant
16 patronising: treating s.o. in a friendly way but still showing you think you are better
17 delineation [dɪˌlɪniˈeɪʃən]: manner of describing s.o. or s.th.
18 deceptive: misleading, making you believe s.th. that is not true
19 stock: ancestry

Price Warung (1855–1911)

Price Warung, whose actual name was William Astley, was born in Liverpool England, and immigrated to Australia with his parents in 1859. After finishing school in Melbourne, he became a book-seller and journalist known for his radical views. Early in his life he developed an interest in Australian history and the convict[1] system, which he saw as a symbol of the stupidity and cruelty of British imperialism.

Warung's stories of the convict system, one of the important strands of Australian history, first appeared in the anti-imperialist and anti-monarchist literary magazine *The Bulletin* from 1890 to 1893. His short stories are characterised by their bitter sarcasm that is reminiscent[2] of his contemporary[3], Joseph Conrad[4].

He died penniless, in poor health, and addicted to[5] drugs.

To quote the author in his preface to his collection of convict stories, **Tales of the Convict System,** 1892:

> The series of stories from which the contents of this book are selected, and which have appeared, with an occasional intermission[6], in the weekly issues of *The Bulletin* during the last two years, are true in essence[7]. There is not one in which the motive has not been suggested by, or based upon, fact. They have been submitted to[8] Australian readers as the first fruits, in literary form, of nearly twenty years' study and investigation of the sources of Australian history,

---

[1] convict: a person found guilty of a crime and sent to prison
[2] reminiscent: reminding you
[3] contemporary: person living at the same time
[4] Joseph Conrad (1857–1924): English writer of Polish origin – cf. his short story, *An Outpost of Progress* in **The Many Voices of English**, Diesterweg
[5] addicted to: unable to stop taking (a drug)
[6] intermission: period of time when s.th. stops for a short time
[7] in essence: in the most important aspects
[8] submitted to: presented to

and, however far his work falls short of the standard of graphic story-telling, the writer feels that he can honestly claim that he has sought to communicate to it the quality of historic truth. His principal aim throughout has been the preservation of the appropriate local colour and the historic atmosphere, and not the mere presentment of dramatic episodes. To this end he has directed analytic research and systematic industry, and if he has erred[9] in his attempts to describe the subjects of The System as men and women, and not as chattels[10] – things – numbers, the fault cannot be attributed to carelessness or to an indifference to the obligations which bind the historian. In some minor instances the writer has intentionally committed himself to anachronisms[11]. This has been done where the precise indication[12] of a transport-ship, a register-number or a date, might have led to the identification of individual transport! or officials. He conceives[13] that the reader is not concerned with the actual personality behind particular characters of his stories, but only with such human interest as he has succeeded in attaching to those unhonoured pioneers of Australian settlement, the convicts.

It has been said by a distinguished Melbourne *littérateur*[14] that the pages which record the penal[15] chapters of Australian history "should be turned down." We cannot turn them down if we would[16]. The Transportation System has knitted[17] itself into the fibres[18] of our national being. There is not a single Australasian province (and this includes Victoria, South Australia and Maoriland[19]) whose character was left unvitiated[20] by the methods England adopted for the disposal[21] of the criminals she had bred[22] [...]

---

9 to err: to make a mistake
10 chattel: a piece of movable property
11 anachronism: s.th. that belongs to another time
12 indication: mentioning
13 to conceive: to believe
14 littérateur (French): author
15 penal ['pi:nəl] having to do with punishment
16 would: wanted to
17 to knit [nɪt] (fig.): (here): to become a very important part of s.th.
18 fibre (fig.): (here): one of the very small parts of s.th. larger
19 Maoriland: an old name for New Zealand
20 unvitiated [ʌn'vɪʃeɪtɪd]: uncorrupted
21 disposal: removal
22 bred: created

Information Box

The Convict System: Also known as "The System," involved the transportation of men and women convicted of crimes (often trivial), who were transported from Great Britain to the Australian colonies from 1787 to 1868. It was considered a convenient way of getting rid of the criminal class. Increasing protests against the cruel and arbitrary treatment of these convicts brought this form of punishment to an end. The convict experience proved to be crucial in the development of the Australian consciousness and a source of much significance for historians and writers.

How Muster-Master[23] Stoneman Earned His Breakfast (1892)

I.

An unpretentious[24] building of rough-hewn[25] stone standing in the middle of a small, stockaded[26] enclosure[27]. A doorway in the wall of the building facing the entrance-gate to the yard. To the left of the doorway, a glazed[28] window of the ordinary size. To its right a paneless[29] aperture[30], so low and narrow that were the four upright and two transverse[31] bars, which grate[32] it, doubled in thickness no interstice[33] would be left for the admission[34] of light or air to the interior. Behind the bars – a face.

Sixteen hours hence[35] that face will look its last upon the world which has stricken[36] it countless cruel blows. In a corner of the enclosure the executioner's hand is even now busy stitching[37] into a shapeless cap, a square of grey serge[38]. Tomorrow the same hand will use the cap to hood[39] the face, as one of the few simple preliminaries[40] to swinging the carcase[41] to which the face is attached from the rude[42] platform now in course of erection[43] against the stockade fence and barely 20 yards in front of the stone building.

---

[23] muster-master: official in a penal colony in charge of keeping the records of the convicts, inspections, buying the supplies, and giving the convicts their tasks or punishment
[24] unpretentious [ˌʌnprɪˈtenʃəs]: simple, unimposing
[25] rough [rʌf]-hewn [hjuːn]: cut into a shape that is not smooth or polished
[26] stockaded: with a wall of strong wooden posts
[27] enclosure: piece of land surrounded by a wall or fence
[28] glazed: with a sheet of glass
[29] paneless: without a sheet of glass
[30] aperture (formal): opening
[31] transverse: crossing from side to side
[32] to grate: to provide with a framework of metal bars
[33] interstice (formal): small space
[34] admission: letting in
[35] hence (formal): in the near future
[36] to stricken: to wound or injure
[37] to stitch: *nähen*
[38] serge [sɛːʤ]: strong cloth made of wool
[39] to hood: to pull over
[40] preliminary (formal): happening before in preparation
[41] carcase [ˈkɑːkeɪs]: dead body (normally of an animal slaughtered for food)
[42] rude: roughly made
[43] erection (formal): being put up

The building is the gaol[44] – locally known as the "cage" – of Oatlands[45], a small township in the midlands of Van Dieman's Land, which has gradually grown up round a convict "muster-station[46]," established by Governor Davey[47]. The time is five o'clock on a September evening, 55 years ago. At nine o'clock on the following morning, Convict Glancy, No. 17,927, transportee[48] *ex*[49] ship Pestonjee Bomanjee[50] (second trip), originally under sentence[51] for seven years for the theft of a silk handkerchief from a London "swell[52]," will suffer the extreme penalty of the law for having, in an intemperate[53] moment, objected to[54] the mild discipline with which a genial[55] and loving motherland had sought to correct his criminal tendencies. In other words, Convict Glancy, metaphorically goaded[56] by the wordy insults and literally by the bayonet-tip of one of his motherland's reformatory agents – to wit[57], Road-gang[58] Overseer James Jones – had scattered[59] J.J.'s brains over a good six square yards[60] of metalled[61] roadway. The deed has been rapturously[62] applauded by Glancy's fellow-gangers, all of whom had the inclination, but lacked the courage, to wield[63] the crowbar[64] that has been the means of erasing this particular tyrant's name from the pay-sheets of His Britannic Majesty's

44 gaol (BE): jail
45 Oatlands: town near Hobart in Van Dieman's Land (now Tasmania) – The penal colonies in Van Dieman's Land had a reputation for extreme cruelty.
46 muster-station: an area where convicts are brought together for punishment or tasks
47 Davey: Thomas Davey (1758–1823) was the largely incompetent Lieutenant-Governor of Van Dieman's Land from 1813 to1816.
48 transportee: transported convict
49 ex (Latin): from
50 Pestonjee Bomanjee: Being a typical Parsi name, the ship – probably owned by a Parsi – originally sailed from Mumbai, India.
51 under sentence: with a punishment decided by a judge
52 swell (old-fashioned): fashionable young man, dandy
53 intemperate: showing lack of control over yourself
54 to object to s.th.: to refuse to accept s.th., to protest against s.th. you are made to do
55 genial: cheerful and kind
56 to goad: to keep annoying s.o. until he or she reacts
57 to wit (formal, law): to be more exact
58 road-gang: a group of convicts who are made to build and repair roads
59 to scatter: to throw in many different directions
60 yard: one yard = 0.9144 m
61 metalled: made of small pieces of stone
62 rapturously: with extreme pleasure
63 to wield [wi:ld]: to make use of a tool or weapon
64 crowbar: a straight iron bar with a curved end, used for forcing open boxes and moving heavy objects

Colonial Penal Establishment. Nevertheless and notwithstanding[65] such tribute of appreciation[66], H.B.M's Colonial representatives, police, judicial, and gubernatorial[67], have thought it rather one to be censured[68] and have, accordingly[69], left Convict Glancy for execution.

This decision of the duly-constituted[70] authorities Convict Glancy has somewhat irrelevantly[71] (as it will seem to us at this enlightened[72] day) acknowledged by a fervent[73] " Thank God!" – an ejaculation[74] rendered[75] the more remarkable by the fact that never before in his convict history had he linked the name of the Deity[76] with any expression of gratitude for the many blessings[77] enjoyed by him in that state of penal servitude[78] to which it had pleased the same Deity to call him[79]. On the contrary, he had constantly indulged in[80] maledictions[81] on his fate and on his Maker[82]. He had resolutely[83] cursed[84] the benignant[85] forces with which the System and the King's Regulations had surrounded him, and he had failed to reverence[86] as he ought the triangles[87], the gang-chains[88], the hominy[89], the prodding[90]

---

65 notwithstanding (formal): however
66 such tribute of appreciation: i.e. the approval and happiness felt by the convicts because James Jones had been killed
67 gubernatorial: having to do with the governor
68 to censure: (ironic) to criticise harshly
69 accordingly: therefore
70 duly-constituted: legally established
71 irrelevantly: in a way that does not seem to fit with the situation
72 enlightened: *aufgeklärt*
73 fervent: showing strong and sincere feelings
74 ejaculation (formal): sudden sound or shout made when angry or surprised
75 rendered: made
76 the Deity (formal): God
77 blessing: *Segen*
78 penal servitude: condition of having no freedom because of being a convict
79 to call him: (here): to assign him (*zuteilen*)
80 to indulge in s.th.: to allow yourself to have or do s.th. that you like, but considered bad for you
81 malediction (formal): curse (*Fluch*)
82 Maker: the Creator, God
83 resolutely: with great determination
84 to curse: *verfluchen*
85 benignant: kind and gracious as a king to his subjects
86 to reverence: to show great respect
87 triangle: three long, thick pieces of wood stuck in the ground and joined together at the top at which the hands of a convict were tied when he or she was to be whipped
88 gang-chains: chains that connected the legs of convicts working in a road-gang
89 hominy: dried maize boiled in water or milk
90 to prod: to push s.o. with a pointed object

bayonet, and the other things which would have conduced[91] to his reformation, had he but manifested[92] a more humble[93] and obedient spirit. No wonder, therefore, as Chaplain[94] Ford said, that it has come about that he[95] has qualified for the capital doom[96].

Upon this doom, in so far as it could be represented by the gallows[97], Convict Glancy was now gazing[98] with an unflinching[99] eye. On this September evening he stands at his cell-window looking on half-a-dozen brown-clothed figures handling saw, and square[100], and hammer, as they fix in the earth two sturdy[101] uprights[102], and to those a projecting cross-beam[103]; as they bind the two with a solid tie-piece[104] of knotless[105] hardwood; as they build a narrow platform of planks[106] around the gallows-tree ; as they fasten a rope to the notched[107] end of the cross-beam; and as they slope[108] to the edge of the planks, ten feet from the ground, a rude[109] ladder. All the drowsy[110] afternoon he had watched the working party, though Chaplain Ford had stood by his side droning[111] of the grace[112] which had been withheld[113] from him in life, but might still be his in death. He[114] had felt interested, had Convict Glancy, in these prepara-

---

91 to conduce: to lead or contribute
92 to manifest (formal): to demonstrate, to show
93 humble: *demütig*
94 chaplain ['tʃæplɪn]: a priest or minister who takes care of the religious needs of people in the armed forces, prison, or hospital
95 he: i.e. Glancy
96 capital doom (terrible event): i.e. capital punishment (*Todesstrafe*)
97 gallows: *Galgen*
98 to gaze: to stare
99 unflinching: determined, steadfast
100 square: an instrument in the shape of a T or L used to test right angles
101 sturdy: strong and not easily damaged
102 upright: (here): a long and thick vertical piece of wood
103 projecting cross-beam: a long, thick connecting piece of wood that sticks out
104 tie-piece: a piece of wood that connects two other pieces of wood
105 knotless: without a knot (a hard round spot in a piece of wood where there was once a branch)
106 plank: a long, narrow, flat piece of wood used for making floors
107 notched: with a v-shaped cut in the surface
108 to slope: (here): to place s.th. – e.g. a ladder against a wall or other surface – at an angle other than a right angle
109 rude: (here) not carefully made
110 drowsy: making you feel relaxed and tired
111 to drone: (here): to constantly say s.th. in a low, monotonous voice
112 grace: *Gnade*
113 to withhold: to keep back, to not allow to have
114 he: i.e. Glancy

tions for the event in which he was to act such a prominent[115] part on the morrow[116]. He had even laughed at the grim[117] humour of one of the brown-garbed[118] workers who, when the warder[119]'s eye was off him, had gone through the pantomime of noosing[120] the rope-end round his own neck – a little joke which contributed much to the (necessarily noiseless) delight of the rest of the gang.

Altogether, Convict Glancy reflected[121] as dusk fell[122], and the working party gathered up their tools, and the setting sun tipped[123] the bayonets of the guard with a diamond iridescence[124], that he had spent many a duller[125] afternoon. If the Chaplain had only held his tongue, the time would have passed with real pleasantness. He said as much to the good man as the latter[126] remarked to the warder on duty[127] in the cell that he would look in again after supper.

"You may save yourself the trouble, sir," quoth[128], respectfully enough, Convict Glancy. "You have spoilt my last afternoon. Don't spoil my last night!"

Chaplain Ford winced[129] at the words. He was still comparatively new to the work of spiritually superintending[130] a hundred or so monsters who looked upon the orthodox hell[131] as a place where residence would be pleasantly recreative[132] after Port Arthur Settlement[133] and Norfolk

---

115 prominent: important
116 on the morrow (archaic): the next day
117 grim: harshly ironic
118 garbed (formal): dressed
119 warder: a person who guards prisoners or convicts
120 to noose: to form into a noose (*Schlinge*)
121 to reflect: to think deeply about
122 as dusk fell: as the sunlight disappeared and it became dark
123 tipped: (here): caused the tips of the bayonets to shine
124 iridescence: the quality of showing many bright colours at the same time
125 dull: boring
126 the latter: i.e. the chaplain
127 on duty: *im Dienst*
128 to quoth (archaic): to say
129 to wince: to make a sudden expression on your face to show pain or embarrassment
130 to superintend (formal): to be in charge of s.th. and make sure that everything is working, being done as it should be
131 orthodox hell: the hell as described by the Church of England, the Roman Catholic Church, or other established churches
132 recreative: pleasant and enjoyable
133 Port Arthur Settlement: a penal station in Van Diemen's Land from 1833 until the 1850s – The hardest of convicted British criminals and second offenders were sent there. It was known for being especially harsh and cruel.

Island[134]; and the time lay still in the future when, being completely embruted[135], he would come to regard it as a very curious circumstance[136] indeed that Christ had omitted[137] eulogistic[138] reference to the System from the Sermon on the Mount[139]. Consequently[140], he winced and sighed[141], not so much – to do him justice[142] – at the utter[143] depravity[144] of Convict Glancy as at his own inability to reach the reprobate[145]'s heart. But he took the hint; he mournfully[146] said he would not return that evening, but would be with the prisoner by half-past 5 o'clock in the morning.

II.

When Chaplain Ford entered the enclosure immediately before the hour he had named, he at once understood, from the excitement manifested by a group assembled in front of the "cage," that something was amiss[147]. Voices were uttering[148] fearful words, impetuously[149], almost shriekingly[150], and hands swung lanterns – the grey dawn had not yet driven the darkness from the stockade – and brandished[151] muskets[152] furiously[153]. A

---

134 Norfolk Island: an island north of New Zealand that was used as a penal settlement from 1824 to 1854 – Convicts who were never to be freed again were sent there. It was the worst of the penal colonies.
135 embruted: hardened, brutal, like a beast
136 circumstance: the conditions and facts that are connected with and affect a situation
137 to omit: to leave out
138 eulogistic: praising very much
139 Sermon on the Mount: *die Bergpredigt*
140 consequently: therefore
141 to sigh [saɪ]: *seufzen*
142 to do him justice: to treat him fairly
143 utter: complete
144 depravity [dɪˈprævəti]: state of total moral corruption
145 reprobate (formal): immoral person
146 mournfully: very sadly
147 amiss: wrong
148 to utter: to say s.th.
149 impetuously: impulsively, in a way done quickly without thinking first
150 shriekingly: with high, loud screams
151 to brandish: to hold and wave about in a threatening way
152 musket: a smoothbore (*mit glattem Lauf*), heavy shoulder firearm that at the time was already outdated – It had to be loaded in the front, was not very accurate, and had a short range.
153 furiously: (here): excitedly

very brief space of time served to inform the reverend functionary[154] what had gone wrong.

Convict Glancy had made his escape, having previously murdered, with the victim's own bayonet, the warder who had been told off[155] to watch him during the night. This latter circumstance[156] was, of course, unfortunate, but alone it would not have created the excitement, for the murder of prison officials was a common enough occurrence. It was the other thing that galled[157] the gesticulating and blaspheming[158] group. That a prisoner, fettered[159] with ten-pound irons[160], should have broken out of gaol on the very eve of[161] his execution – why, it was calculated to shake the confidence of the Comptroller-General[162] himself in the infallibility[163] and perfect righteousness[164] of the System. And, popular and authoritative belief in the System once shattered[165], where would they be?

The murdered man had gone on duty at 10 o'clock, and very shortly afterwards he must have met with his fate. How Glancy had obtained possession of the bayonet could only be conjectured[166]. As was the custom during the day or two preceding a convict's execution, he had been left unmanacled[167], and ironed[168] with double leg-chains only. Thus his hands were free to perpetrate[169] the deed once he grasped the weapon. Glancy, on his escape, had taken the instrument with him, but there was no doubt that he had inflicted[170] death with it, the wound in the dead man's breast being obviously caused by the regulation bayonet. Possibly the sentinel[171]

---

154 reverend (title used for religious ministers) functionary (official) (ironic, jocular): i.e. the minister, Chaplain Ford
155 to tell off: to give s.o. a task
156 latter circumstance: i.e. the warder being killed with his own bayonet
157 to gall [gɔ:l]: to make s.o. feel angry and upset
158 to blaspheme [ˌblæsˈfi:m]: to swear using the name of God or holy things
159 to fetter: to bind the bottom part of the legs with chains or other heavy objects
160 irons: chains or other heavy objects made of iron
161 on the very eve of: the evening just before
162 Comptroller-General: the head of finances
163 infallibility: the condition of never making a mistake
164 righteousness: being morally right and justifiable
165 to shatter (fig.): to suddenly break into pieces
166 to conjecture (formal): to guess
167 unmanacled: without manacles (*Handfesseln*)
168 to iron: (here): to fetter
169 to perpetrate (formal): to perform, to be responsible for
170 to inflict: to make s.o. suffer s.th. unpleasant
171 sentinel: soldier whose job it is to watch over s.th./s.o.

had nodded[172], and then a violent wrench[173] of the prisoner's wrist and a sudden stab[174] had extended[175] his momentary slumber[176] into an eternal[177] sleep. The bayonet had also been used by Glancy to prise up[178] a flooring-flag[179], and to scoop out[180] an aperture under the wall, the base-stones of which, following the slipshod[181] architecture of the time, rested on the surface and were not sunk into the ground.

The work of excavation[182] must have taken the convict several hours, and must have been conducted as noiselessly as the manner of committing the crime itself. A solitary[183] warder occupied the outer guardroom, but he asserted[184] that he had heard no sound except the exchange of whistle-signals between the dormitory guard[185] at the convict-barracks (a quarter-of-mile away at the rear of[186] the gaol-stockade) and the military patrol. The night routine of the "cage" did not insist upon the whistle-signal between the men on duty, but they passed a simple "All's well" every hour. And this the guardroom-warder maintained he had done with the officer inside the condemned cell[187], the response being given in a low tone, from consideration[188], so the former[189] thought, for the sleeping convict so soon to die. Of course, if this man was to be believed, Glancy must have uttered the words. It was not the first time the signal which should have been given by a prison officer had been made by his convict murderer.

The murder was discovered on the arrival of the relief watch[190] at five o'clock. The last "All's well" was exchanged at four. Consequently, the

---

172 to nod: to fall asleep
173 wrench: a sudden, violent twist or pull
174 stab: suddenly pushing a knife or other sharp instrument into a person's body
175 to extend: to make s.th. last longer
176 slumber: peaceful sleep
177 eternal: *ewig*
178 to prise up: to force open
179 flooring-flag: a large, flat, square piece of stone that is used for floors
180 to scoop out: to dig out a small amount of s.th.
181 slipshod: careless
182 excavation [ˌekskəˈveɪʃən]: (here): the act of digging
183 solitary: single
184 to assert: to maintain (*behaupten*)
185 dormitory guard: guard responsible for the sleeping quarters
186 at the rear of: behind
187 the condemned cell: i.e. the cell with the condemned (sentenced to die) man inside
188 from consideration: thinking of the feelings or condition of another person
189 the former: i.e. the warder in the outer guardroom
190 relief-watch: guard or guards who replace another guard or guards

escapee had less than an hour's start. The scaling[191] of the stockade would not be difficult even for a man in irons, and once in the bush an experienced hand would soon find a method of fracturing[192] the links.

It must be admitted that this contumacious[193] proceeding[194] of Convict Glancy was most vexatious[195]. Under-Sheriff Ropewell, now soundly[196] reposing[197] at the township[198] inn[199], would be forthcoming[200] at 9 o'clock with his Excellency[201]'s warrant[202] in his hand to demand from Muster-Master Stoneman the body of one James Glancy, and Muster-Master Stoneman would have to apologise for his inability to produce the said body. The difficulty was quite unprecedented[203], and Stoneman, as he stood in the midst of his minions[204], groaned[205] audibly[206] at the prospect[207] of having to do the thing most abhorrent[208] to the official mind – establish a precedent[209].

"Such a thing was never heard of!" he cried. "A man to bolt[210] just when he was to be turned off[211]! And the d – d[212] hypocrite[213] tried to make his Honor[214] and all of us think that he was only too happy to be scragged[215]. It's too d – d bad!"

---

191 scaling: climbing to the top of s.th. high
192 to fracture: to break a hard material
193 contumacious [ˌkɒːntjuˈmeɪʃəs] (formal): showing no respect for authority
194 proceeding (formal): activity
195 vexatious [vekˈseɪʃəs] (formal): upsetting, annoying
196 soundly: very deeply
197 to repose: to sleep peacefully
198 township: small town or village
199 inn: small hotel with a restaurant
200 forthcoming: about to appear
201 his Excellency: the judge
202 warrant: legal document signed by a judge
203 unprecedented: never having happened before
204 minion (jocular): (here): unimportant official
205 to groan: *stöhnen*
206 audibly: in a way that can be heard
207 prospect: possibility, probability
208 abhorrent (formal): awful
209 to establish a precedent: to do s.th. that was never done officially before
210 to bolt: to run away
211 to turn off (colloquial): normally (BE): to fire s.o., (here): to execute
212 d – d: damned
213 hypocrite [ˈhɪpəkrɪt]: *Heuchler*
214 Honor: a high official or judge
215 to scrag (colloquial): to hang at the neck

It certainly did seem peculiar that Glancy, who had apparently much rejoiced[216] at the contemplation[217] of his early decease[218], should give leg-bail[219] just when he was to realise his wishes. He had told the judge that "he was d – d glad they were going to kill him right off instead of by inches," and yet he had voluntarily thrown off the noose[220] when it was virtually[221] round his neck. Was it the mere contrariness[222] of the convict nature that prompted[223] the escape? Or, was it the innate[224] love of life that becomes stronger as the benefits[225] of living become fewer and fewer. Had the craving[226] for existence and for freedom surged over[227] his despair and recklessness[228] at the eleventh hour?

Such were the enquiries[229] which Chaplain Ford put to himself as, horrified, he took in[230] the particulars[231] of No. 17,927's crowning enormities[232] from the hubbub[233] of the group.

"Damn it!" said the Muster-Master at last, "we are losing time. The devil can't have gone far with those ten-pounders on him. We'll have to put the regulars[234] on the track[235] as well as our own men. Warder Briggs, report to Captain White at the barracks, and – "

Muster-Master Stoneman stopped short. Through the foggy air there came the familiar sound as of a convict dragging his irons. What could it

---

216 to rejoice: to express great happiness about s.th.
217 contemplation: deep thought
218 decease (formal): death
219 to give leg-bail (colloquial): to escape on foot – Normally, bail (*Kaution*) is money you pay to a judge during a trial instead of going to jail.
220 noose: *Schlinge*
221 virtually: just about
222 contrariness: unexpected behaviour, willingness to start a conflict
223 to prompt: to cause
224 innate: inborn, existing since birth
225 benefit: advantage, useful effect
226 craving: strong desire
227 to surge over (fig.): to suddenly dominate, to overpower
228 recklessness: quality of not thinking of the dangers and possible results of your actions
229 enquiry (formal): question
230 to take in: to find out about
231 particulars: details
232 crowning enormities (plural): incredible and unusual crime
233 hubbub: loud sound made by several people talking at the same time
234 regulars: (here): soldiers from the British armed forces
235 track: *Fährte*, *Spur*

be! No prisoners had been as yet loosed[236] from the dormitory. Whence[237] could the noise proceed?

Clink – clank – s-sh – dr-g-g – clink – clank – dr-g-g. The sound drew nearer, and Convict Glancy turned in at the enclosure gateway – unescorted[238]. He had severed[239] the leg-chain at the link which connected with the basil[240] of the left ankle, but had not taken the trouble to remove the other part of the chain. Thus, while he could take his natural pace[241] with his left foot, he dragged the fetters[242] behind his right leg.

A moment of hushed surprise, and then three or four men rushed towards him. The first who touched him he felled[243] with a blow[244].

"Not yet," said he, grimly[245]. "I give myself up, Mr. Stoneman – you don't take me! I give myself up – you ain't going to get ten quid[246] for taking me." And then Convict Glancy laughed, and held out his hands for the handcuffs[247]. He laughed more heartily[248] as the subordinate[249] hirelings[250] of the System threw themselves upon him like hounds[251] on their prey[252].

"No need to turn out[253] the sodgers[254] now, Muster-Master – not till nine o'clock." Once more his hideous[255] laugh rang through the yards. "You had an easier job than you expected, hadn't you, Stoneman, old cove[256]?"

---

236 to loose: to free, to release
237 whence (formal): from where
238 unescorted: (here): without a guard
239 to sever: to cut s.th. off s.th.
240 basil: ankle (*Fußgelenk*) irons
241 pace: speed
242 fetters: chains and other heavy objects
243 to fell: to cause to fall
244 blow: *Schlag*
245 grimly: in a way sounding and looking very serious
246 ten quid: the reward of ten pounds paid by the Government on the recapture of an escaped prisoner (author's explanation)
247 handcuffs: *Handschellen*
248 heartily: with enjoyment and pleasure
249 subordinate: in a lower position
250 hireling: a person who is willing to do anything or work for anyone as long as he/she is paid for it
251 hound: a dog used for hunting
252 prey [preɪ]: an animal that is hunted
253 to turn out: to order to appear
254 sodger (dialect): soldier
255 hideous: very unpleasant
256 cove (old-fashioned, BE and Australian English): fellow, chap

Muster-Master Stoneman had been surprised into silence and into an unusual abstinence[257] from blasphemy by the re-appearance – quite unprecedented under the circumstances! – of the doomed[258] wretch[259]. But the desperado[260]'s jeering[261] tones whipped[262] him into speech.

"Curse you[263] !" he yelled[264]. "I'll teach you to laugh on the other side of your mouth presently. You'd better have kept away." He literally[265] foamed[266] in his mad anger.

"Do you think I couldn't have stopped away[267] if I'd wanted to, having got clear[268]?" A lofty[269] scorn[270] rang out in the words. "But do you think I was going to run away when I was so near Freedom as that?" And the wretch jerked[271] his manacled hands in the direction of the gallows. "You d – d fool!"

No one spoke for a full half-minute. Then:" Why did you break[272] gaol then?" asked the Muster-Master.

"*Because I wanted to spit[273] on Jones' grave!*" was the reply.

III.

Muster-Master Stoneman was as good as his word. Death couldn't drive the smile from Glancy's face. That could only be done by one thing – the lash[274].

---

257 abstinence: *Enthaltsamkeit*
258 doomed: soon to die
259 wretch [retʃ]: a person you feel great pity for
260 desperado: a desperate person ready to commit a violent crime
261 to jeer: to laugh and make rude remarks to a person to show a lack of respect
262 to whip (fig.): to cause s.o. to react quickly and violently
263 Curse you!: *Verflucht*!
264 to yell: to shout very loudly
265 literally: indeed, really
266 to foam: *schäumen*
267 stopped away: stopped to rest somewhere far away
268 clear: safe and far enough away
269 lofty: arrogant
270 scorn: *Verachtung*
271 to jerk: to move with a sudden, short, sharp movement
272 to break: to escape from
273 to spit: *spucken*
274 lash: the thin leather part of a whip

When next the Muster-Master spoke it was to order the prisoner a double ration of cocoa[275] and bread. And, "Briggs," he continued, "while he is getting it, see that the triangles are rigged[276]."

"The triangles, sir!" exclaimed Officer Briggs and Convict Glancy together.

"I said the triangles, and I mean the triangles. No. 17,927 has broken gaol, and as Muster-Master of this station, and governor of this gaol, and as a magistrate[277] of the territory, I can give him 750 lashes[278] for escaping. But as he has to go through another little ceremony this morning I'll let him off with a 'canary'[279]."

"You surely cannot mean it, sir!" exclaimed Parson Ford.

"Mean it, sir! By G –[280], I'll show you I mean it," replied the M.M., whose blaspheming no presence restrained[281] save[282] that of his official superiors. "Give him the cocoa. Warder Tuff, give the doctor my compliments[283], and tell him his attendance is required here. Tell him he'd better bring his smelling-salts – they may be wanted," he sneered[284] in conclusion[285].

"You devil!" cried Glancy. The reckless[286] grin passed away, and his face faded[287] to the pallor[288] of the death he was so soon to die.

As Muster-Master Stoneman turned on his heel to prepare the warrant for the flogging[289], he looked at his watch. It was half-past six.

---

[275] cocoa ['kəʊkəʊ]: a hot drink made by mixing cocoa powder with milk or water and sugar

[276] to rig: to set up

[277] magistrate: judge in the lowest courts

[278] lash: a hit with a whip

[279] a canary (colloquial, Australian English): a hundred lashes – Muster-Master Stoneman had doubtless in his mind's eye when he made this remark the decision of a Sydney Court, which had legalised the infliction [punishment], by an official holding a plurality of offices of a sentence passed by him in each capacity, but for the one offence. (author's comment) – i.e. a person with a number of official positions cannot give a criminal the same number of punishments as he has positions for one crime committed.

[280] G –: God

[281] to restrain: to stop s.o. from doing s.th.

[282] save: except for

[283] compliments: good wishes

[284] to sneer: to smile in a way showing no respect, to mock

[285] in conclusion: as the final remark

[286] reckless: not caring about the dangers or results of what you do

[287] to fade: to become less bright

[288] pallor: pale colouring

[289] flogging: punishment with a whip or stick

At seven o'clock the first lash from the cat-o'-nine-tails[290] fell upon Convict Glancy's back.

At 7.30 his groaning and bleeding body, which had received the full hundred of flaying stripes[291], lay on the pallet[292] of the cell where he had murdered the night-guard but a few hours before.

At eight o'clock Executioner Johnson entered the cell. "I've brought yer sumthink to 'arden yer[293], Glancy, ol'[294] man. I'll rub it in, an' it'll help yer to keep up[295]." So tender[296] a sympathy inspired Mr. Johnson's words that anyone not knowing him would have thought he was the bearer[297] of some priceless balsam[298]. But Convict Glancy knew him; and, maddened by pain though he was, had still sensibility[299] enough left to make a shuddering[300] resistance to the hangman as he proceeded to rub into the gashed[301] flesh a handful of coarse[302] salt. "By the Muster-Master's orders, sonny[303]," soothingly[304] remarked Johnson. "To 'arden yer."

At 8.45 Under-Sheriff Ropewell, who had been apprised[305] while at breakfast of the murder and escape, appeared on the scene escorted[306] by his javelin-men[307]. This gentleman, too, had been greatly perplexed[308] by Convict Glancy's proceedings. "Really it was most inconsiderate[309] of the man," he said to the Muster-Master. "I do not know whether I ought to proceed to execution, pending[310] his trial for this second murder."

---

290 cat-o'-nine-tails: a whip made of nine strings with knots in them
291 flaying stripes: the marks left by the strings of the whip with some of the skin gone, too
292 pallet: straw-filled bed
293 ... yer ... yer: you s.th. to harden you
294 ol': old
295 to keep up: to stand up straight
296 tender: affectionate, expressing warm feelings
297 bearer: a person who brings s.th. with him
298 balsam ['bɔːlsəm]: oil obtained from trees or plants to heal wounds
299 sensibility: awareness, ability to notice your surroundings
300 to shudder: to shake because of being cold or frightened
301 gashed: with deep cuts
302 coarse [kɔːs]: not fine, with relatively large pieces
303 sonny (colloquial): young man
304 soothingly: in a way to make s.o. less worried or upset
305 to apprise (formal): to inform
306 escorted: accompanied
307 javelin-men: soldiers or police with long and sharp bayonets – For close fighting, long and sharp bayonets were necessary until the late 1860s as it took too long to load and reload rifles and muskets from the front of the barrel (*Lauf*).
308 to perplex: to confuse
309 inconsiderate: thoughtless
310 pending: while waiting for

"Oh," said the latter functionary – flicking[311] with his handkerchief from his coat-sleeve, as he spoke, a drop of Convict Glancy's blood that had fallen there from a reflex[312] swirl[313] of the lash, "I think your duty is clear. You must hang him at nine o'clock, and try[314] him afterwards for the last crime."

And as Convict Glancy, per[315] Pestonjee Bomanjee (second), No. 17,927, was punctually hanged at 9.05, it is to be presumed[316] that the Under-Sheriff had accepted this solution of the difficulty.

At 10.15 a mass of carrion[317] having been huddled[318] into a shell[319], and certain formalities, which in the estimation[320] of the System served as efficiently as a coroner's inquest[321], having been duly[322] attended to[323], Muster-Master Stoneman bethought himself [324] that he had not breakfasted.

"I'll see you later, Mr. Ropewell," he said, as the latter was endorsing[325] the Governor's warrant with the sham[326] verdict[327]; "I'm going to breakfast. I think I've earned it this morning."

---

[311] to flick: to remove with a quick movement
[312] reflex: happening without being able to control, automatic
[313] swirl: the movement of s.th. that twists and turns in different directions
[314] to try: to bring before a court of law
[315] per (Latin): (here): brought with
[316] to presume: to assume (*annehmen*)
[317] carrion: dead and rotting meat
[318] to huddle: to place carelessly
[319] shell: primitive coffin (*Sarg*)
[320] estimation (formal): judgement, opinion
[321] coroner's inquest: the official determination of the cause of death
[322] duly: according to the rules and regulations
[323] to attend to (formal): to take care of (*erledigen*)
[324] to bethink yourself (archaic): to remind yourself
[325] to endorse: to provide a document with an additional signature
[326] sham: false
[327] verdict: decision, judgement, or conclusion

1. Explain the title of the short story.

2. Comment or the characters' names.

3. What different registers are used in the short story? Why?

4. Make a table with the sentences that have a very unusual structure. Simplify them. What seems more effective?

5. From what viewpoint is the short story told?

6. What is the author trying to convey to the reader? Where do his sympathies lie? Explain. Does he achieve the objective stated in his preface (pp. 7–8)?

7. Why do you think this short story is still so popular?

8. Research the prison system in your country.

9. Discuss the pros and cons of capital punishment.

For further reading:

Tales of the Convict System by Price Warung, 1892, available as a reprint from Bibliobazaar
The Fatal Shore by Robert Hughes, Alfred A. Knopf, Inc., New York, 1987 – well-researched and readable history of the Convict System – Robert Hughes criticises Price Warung and other contemporary Australian writers for exaggerating and sensationalising the brutality of the Convict System.

Henry Lawson (1867–1922)

Henry Lawson was born on the goldfields of Grenfell, New South Wales. He became totally deaf at the age of 14. Because of constant conflicts between his parents, his childhood was an unhappy one. His first work of short fiction appeared in the anti-imperialist literary magazine *The Bulletin* in 1888. After travelling to New Zealand and around Australia, he married Bertha Bredt in 1896. Though experiencing a failed marriage, facing financial ruin, and suffering from mental illness, he continued to publish numerous collections of short stories and poems to the end of his life. On the basis of his own observations and experiences, he produced works that often focused on bush life and the urban poor. On his death Lawson was given a state funeral, the first Australian writer to be so honoured. He is regarded by some as Australia's most important writer.

In the late 19th century Australians began to develop a nationalist self-image that saw a dominant male role as something desirable ("masculinity") with "mateship" being the idea of male solidarity that excluded women. They were either distrusted or assigned the stereotyped role of stoically[1] accepting the hardships of childbearing and domestic work in a frontier society. It is a tribute to the artistry of Henry Lawson that the following short story has become one of the most read Australian short stories, no doubt because it goes beyond nationalism, "masculinity," and "mateship:" A great complexity of thought lies beneath the surface of a tale about a lone woman and her children struggling against a hostile bush country environment. *The Drover's Wife* was first published in *The Bulletin* in 1892.

[1] stoically: without complaining, without protest

The Drover[2]'s Wife (1892)

The two-roomed house is built of round timber[3], slabs[4], and stringy-bark[5], and floored with split[6] slabs. A big bark[7] kitchen standing at one end is larger than the house itself, veranda included.

Bush[8] all round – bush with no horizon, for the country is flat. No ranges[9] in the distance. The bush consists of stunted[10], rotten[11] native[12] apple trees. No undergrowth[13]. Nothing to relieve[14] the eye save[15] the darker green of a few she-oaks[16] which are sighing[17] above the narrow, almost waterless creek[18]. Nineteen miles to the nearest sign of civilisation – a shanty[19] on the main road.

The drover, an ex-squatter[20], is away with sheep. His wife and children are left here alone.

Four ragged[21], dried-up-looking children are playing about the house. Suddenly one of them yells[22]: "Snake[23]! Mother, here's a snake!"

---

2 drover: a person whose job it is to drive sheep or cattle to and from market
3 timber: wood that is used for building houses
4 slab: a thick, flat piece of wood
5 stringy-bark: any of several eucalyptus trees having a bark (*Rinde*) with fibres
6 split: cut along down the middle
7 bark: made of stringy-bark
8 bush: unsettled land covered with small bushes
9 range: a series or chain of mountains
10 stunted: not having been able to achieve the full size
11 rotten: *faul*
12 native: (here): originating from Australia, not imported
13 undergrowth: plants or bushes that grow close to the ground
14 to relieve: to reduce an unpleasant feeling
15 save: except for
16 she-oak: an Australian tree with small leafless branches that are joined together
17 to sigh: *seufzen*
18 creek (AE, Australian English): small stream
19 shanty (Australian English): a primitive pub
20 ex-squatter: a former squatter – squatter: In former times in Australia: a person permitted to live on a piece of public land that belonged to the Crown (the British government)
21 ragged: wearing old and torn clothes
22 to yell: to shout very loudly
23 snake: probably a *Pseudechis australis* (mulga snake) – Very widespread in Australia, its bite is fatal without immediate treatment. It ranges in colour from light brown to black, and can attain a length of 3 meters.

The gaunt[24], sun-browned bushwoman dashes[25] from the kitchen, snatches[26] her baby from the ground, holds it on her left hip[27], and reaches for a stick.

"Where is it?"

"Here! gone into the wood heap[28]!" yells the eldest boy – a sharp-faced urchin[29] of eleven. "Stop there, mother! I'll have him. Stand back! I'll have the beggar[30]."

"Tommy, come here, or you'll be bit[31]. Come here at once when I tell you, you little wretch[32]!"

The youngster comes reluctantly[33], carrying a stick bigger than himself. Then he yells, triumphantly:

"There it goes – under the house!" and darts[34] away with club[35] uplifted. At the same time the big, black, yellow-eyed dog-of-all-breeds[36], who has shown the wildest interest in the proceedings[37], breaks his chain and rushes after that snake. He is a moment late, however, and his nose reaches the crack in the slabs just as the end of its tail disappears. Almost at the same moment the boy's club comes down and skins[38] the aforesaid[39] nose. Alligator takes small notice of this, and proceeds[40] to undermine[41] the building; but he is subdued[42] after a struggle and chained up. They cannot afford to lose him.

The drover's wife makes the children stand together near the doghouse while she watches for the snake. She gets two small dishes of milk and sets

---

[24] gaunt [gɔ:nt]: thin because of not having enough food
[25] to dash: to rush
[26] to snatch: to take quickly, to grab
[27] hip: *Hüfte*
[28] heap: mass of material gathered together, pile
[29] urchin (old-fashioned): dirty, poor and ragged child (*Gassenkind*)
[30] beggar (ironic, jocular): fellow
[31] bit: bitten
[32] wretch: miserable person
[33] reluctantly: unwillingly
[34] to dart: to move quickly
[35] club: a heavy stick with one end thicker than the other
[36] breed: *Züchtung*
[37] proceedings (plural): event or series of events
[38] to skin: to take the skin off
[39] aforesaid: mentioned before
[40] to proceed: to go on
[41] to undermine: (here): to dig under a building so as to decrease its stability
[42] to subdue: to bring s.th./s.o. under control with the use of force

them down near the wall to tempt[43] it to come out; but an hour goes by and it does not show itself.

It is near sunset, and a thunderstorm is coming. The children must be brought inside. She will not take them into the house, for she knows the snake is there, and may at any moment come up through a crack in the rough[44] slab floor; so she carries several armfuls of firewood into the kitchen, and then takes the children there. The kitchen has no floor – or, rather, an earthen one – called a "ground floor" in this part of the bush. There is a large, roughly made table in the centre of the place. She brings the children in, and makes them get on this table. They are two boys and two girls – mere[45] babies. She gives them some supper, and then, before it gets dark, she goes into the house, and snatches up some pillows and bedclothes – expecting to see or lay her hand on the snake any minute. She makes a bed on the kitchen table for the children, and sits down beside it to watch all night.

She has an eye on the corner, and a green sapling[46] club laid in readiness on the dresser[47] by her side; also her sewing basket[48] and a copy of the *Young Ladies' Journal*[49]. She has brought the dog into the room.

Tommy turns in[50], under protest, but says he'll lie awake all night and smash[51] that blinded[52] snake.

His mother asks him how many times she has told him not to swear[53].

He has his club with him under the bedclothes, and Jacky protests.

"Mummy! Tommy's skinnin'[54] me alive wif[55] his club. Make him take it out."

---

[43] to tempt: *in Versuchung bringen* The poisonous snake would not be tempted to come out because of the milk, because snakes of this kind don't drink milk.
[44] rough [rʌf]: having an irregular surface, not smooth
[45] mere: just, only
[46] sapling: made from a young tree
[47] dresser: piece of furniture with drawers to keep clothes in
[48] sewing basket: *Nähkorb*
[49] *Young Ladies' Journal*: magazine published in London in the 19th century with illustrations of the latest women's fashion, suggestions for knitting, cooking, etc.
[50] to turn in: to go to bed for the night
[51] to smash: to hit very hard and break
[52] blinded: i.e. instead of using *God damned* or *bloody*
[53] to swear: *fluchen*
[54] skinnin': skinning
[55] wif: with

Tommy: "Shet[56] up, you little – D'yer[57] want to be bit[58] with[59] the snake?"

Jacky shuts up.

"If yer bit[60]," says Tommy, after a pause, "you'll swell up[61], an' smell, an' turn red an' green an' blue all over till yer[62] bust[63]. Won't he, mother?"

"Now then, don't frighten the child. Go to sleep," she says.

The two younger children go to sleep, and now and then Jacky complains of being "skeezed[64]." More room is made for him. Presently Tommy says: "Mother! listen to them (adjective[65]) little possums[66]. I'd like to screw[67] their blanky[68] necks."

And Jacky protests drowsily[69].

"But they don't hurt us, the little blanks[70]!"

Mother: "There, I told you you'd teach Jacky to swear." But the remark makes her smile. Jacky goes to sleep.

Presently Tommy asks:

"Mother! Do you think they'll ever extricate[71] the (adjective[72]) kangaroo?"

"Lord! How am I to know, child? Go to sleep."

"Will you wake me if the snake comes out?"

"Yes. Go to sleep."

Near midnight. The children are all asleep and she sits there still, sewing and reading by turns. From time to time she glances round the floor and wall plate[73], and, whenever she hears a noise, she reaches for the stick. The thunderstorm comes on, and the wind, rushing through the cracks in the

[56] shet: shut
[57] D'yer ...: Do you
[58] bit: bitten
[59] with: by
[60] yer bit: you are bitten
[61] to swell up: *schwellen*
[62] yer: you
[63] to bust (colloquial): to burst or break
[64] skeezed: squeezed (to squeeze: to press firmly)
[65] adjective: The author wishes to leave out the swear word.
[66] possum: a small American or Australian animal that lives in trees and carries its young in a pouch
[67] to screw: to twist
[68] blanky: Again the author leaves out the swear word.
[69] drowsily: in a way heavy with sleep
[70] blanks: instead of *bloody bastards*
[71] to extricate (formal): to get rid of
[72] adjective: cf. footnote 65
[73] wall plate: thick, horizontal piece of wood along the top of a wall to support the roof

slab[74] wall, threatens to blow out her candle. She places it on a sheltered[75] part of the dresser and fixes up a newspaper to protect it. At every flash of lightning, the cracks between the slabs gleam like polished silver. The thunder rolls, and the rain comes down in torrents[76].

Alligator lies at full length on the floor, with his eyes turned towards the partition[77]. She knows by this that the snake is there. There are large cracks[78] in that wall opening under the floor of the dwelling-house[79].

She is not a coward, but recent events have shaken her nerves. A little son of her brother-in-law[80] was lately bitten by a snake, and died. Besides, she has not heard from her husband for six months, and is anxious about him.

He was a drover, and started squatting[81] here when they were married. The drought[82] of 18– ruined him. He had to sacrifice the remnant[83] of his flock[84] and go droving again. He intends to move his family into the nearest town when he comes back, and, in the meantime, his brother, who keeps a shanty on the main road, comes over about once a month with provisions[85]. The wife has still a couple of cows, one horse, and a few sheep. The brother-in-law kills one of the latter[86] occasionally, gives her what she needs of it, and takes the rest in return for other provisions.

She is used to being left alone. She once lived like this for eighteen months. As a girl she built the usual castles in the air; but all her girlish hopes and aspirations[87] have long been dead. She finds all the excitement and recreation[88] she needs in the *Young Ladies' Journal*, and Heaven help her! takes a pleasure in the fashion-plates[89].

Her husband is an Australian, and so is she. He is careless, but a good enough husband. If he had the means he would take her to the city and

---

[74] slab: a broad, flat, piece of wood
[75] sheltered: protected
[76] in torrents: in large amounts moving quickly
[77] partition: a wall or screen that separates one room from the other
[78] crack: narrow, long opening (*Riss*)
[79] dwelling-house: house you live in
[80] brother-in-law: *Schwager*
[81] to squat (Australia): (here): to establish a home on a piece of land that belongs to the government
[82] drought [draʊt]: period of time when there is relatively little rain – Droughts are frequent in Australia. There were serious droughts in 1877 and from 1880 to 1886.
[83] remnant: what is left or remains
[84] flock: group of sheep
[85] provisions (plural): supplies of food and drink
[86] the latter: i.e. sheep
[87] aspiration: strong desire to achieve s.th.
[88] recreation: activities that contribute to relaxation and enjoyment
[89] fashion-plate: a page with pictures of the latest fashion

keep her there like a princess. They are used to being apart, or at least she is. "No use fretting[90]," she says. He may forget sometimes that he is married; but if he has a good cheque when he comes back he will give most of it to her. When he had money he took her to the city several times – hired[91] a railway sleeping compartment[92], and put up[93] at the best hotels. He also bought her a buggy[94], but they had to sacrifice[95] that along with the rest.

The last two children were born in the bush – one while her husband was bringing a drunken doctor, by force, to attend[96] to her. She was alone on this occasion, and very weak. She had been ill with a fever. She prayed to God to send her assistance. God sent Black Mary[97] – the "whitest[98]" gin[99] in all the land. Or, at least, God sent King[100] Jimmy first, and he sent Black Mary. He put his black face round the doorpost[101], took in the situation[102] at a glance, and said cheerfully: "All right, missus[103] – I bring my old woman, she down alonga[104] creek."

One of the children died while she was here alone. She rode nineteen miles for assistance, carrying the dead child.

It must be near one or two o'clock. The fire is burning low. Alligator lies with his head resting on his paws[105], and watches the wall. He is not a very beautiful dog, and the light shows numerous old wounds where the hair will not grow. He is afraid of nothing on the face of the earth or under it. He will tackle[106] a bullock[107] as readily as he will tackle a flea[108]. He hates

---

90 to fret: to worry, to feel irritated
91 to hire: to rent
92 compartment: *Abteil*
93 to put up: to stay
94 buggy ['bʌgi]: a light carriage for one or two people, pulled by one horse
95 to sacrifice: *opfern*
96 to attend: (here): to treat
97 Black Mary: a typical name that white Australians gave to a female Aborigine
98 white (Australian English): decent
99 gin (Australian English): female Aborigine, (often negative)
100 king (Australian English): (here): male leader of an Aborigine group
101 doorpost: one of the vertical sides of the doorframe
102 took in the situation: observed and made a judgement about the situation
103 missus: form of address if you don't know a woman's name
104 alonga (slang): along a, i.e. beside a
105 paw: foot of a dog or cat (*Pfote*)
106 to tackle: (here): to confront and attack
107 bullock ['bʊlək]: young male cow that has been castrated
108 flea [fli:]: *Floh*

all other dogs – except kangaroo dogs[109] – and has a marked[110] dislike to [sic] friends or relations of the family. They seldom call[111], however. He sometimes makes friends with strangers. He hates snakes and has killed many, but he will be bitten some day and die; most snake dogs end that way.

Now and then the bushwoman lays down her work and watches, and listens, and thinks. She thinks of things in her own life, for there is little else to think about.

The rain will make the grass grow, and this reminds her how she fought a bush fire once while her husband was away. The grass was long, and very dry, and the fire threatened to burn her out. She put on an old pair of her husband's trousers and beat out the flames with a green bough[112], till great drops of sooty[113] perspiration[114] stood out on her forehead and ran in streaks[115] down her blackened arms. The sight of his mother in trousers greatly amused Tommy, who worked like a little hero by her side, but the terrified baby howled[116] lustily[117] for his "mummy." The fire would have mastered[118] her but for four excited bushmen who arrived in the nick of time[119]. It was a mixed-up affair all round; when she went to take up the baby he screamed and struggled convulsively[120], thinking it was a "blackman;" and Alligator, trusting more to the child's sense than his own instinct, charged[121] furiously, and (being old and slightly[122] deaf) did not in his excitement at first recognize his mistress's voice, but continued to hang on to the moleskins[123] until choked off[124] by Tommy with a saddle

---

109 kangaroo dog: an Australian, large, rough-haired dog that resembles a greyhound and is used to hunt kangaroos
110 marked: noticeable, distinct
111 to call: (here): to visit
112 bough [baʊ] (formal): large branch
113 sooty [ˈsʊti]: containing soot (black powder that is produced when wood, coal, etc. is burnt)
114 perspiration: sweat
115 streak: a long, thin, mark or line
116 to howl: to make a long, loud cry
117 lustily: vigorously, strongly
118 to master: to defeat, to overpower
119 in the nick of time: just in time
120 convulsively: suddenly without control, with violent movements
121 to charge: to rush forward and attack
122 slightly: a bit
123 moleskins: trousers made of heavy cotton cloth
124 choked off: forced off the moleskins by placing the strap tightly around the dog's neck so it couldn't breathe properly

strap[125]. The dog's sorrow[126] for his blunder[127], and his anxiety to let it be known that it was all a mistake, was as evident[128] as his ragged[129] tail and a twelve-inch grin[130] could make it. It was a glorious time for the boys; a day to look back to, and talk about, and laugh over for many years.

She thinks how she fought a flood during her husband's absence. She stood for hours in the drenching[131] downpour[132], and dug an overflow gutter[133] to save the dam across the creek. But she could not save it. There are things that a bushwoman cannot do. Next morning the dam was broken, and her heart was nearly broken, too, for she thought how her husband would feel when he came home and saw the result of years of labour swept away. She cried then.

She also fought the *pleuropneumonia*[134] – dosed[135] and bled[136] the few remaining cattle, and wept again when her two best cows died.

Again, she fought a mad bullock that besieged[137] the house for a day. She made bullets and fired at him through cracks in the slabs with an old shotgun[138]. He was dead in the morning. She skinned him and got seventeen-and-six[139] for the hide[140].

She also fights the crows[141] and eagles[142] that have designs on[143] her chickens. Her plan of campaign is very original. The children cry "Crows,

---

125 saddle strap: a long, narrow piece of leather that is placed around the body of a horse to hold a saddle in place

126 sorrow: feeling of great sadness because s.th. bad has happened

127 blunder: stupid mistake

128 evident: clearly seen, obvious

129 ragged [ˈrægɪd]: old, shabby, torn

130 grin: *Grinsen*

131 drenching: making s.th. or s.o. completely wet

132 downpour: heavy rain

133 overflow gutter: a channel in the ground to carry away the flood water

134 pleuropneumonia [plʊərəʊnjuːˈməʊnɪə]: an often fatal illness of the lungs of cows, goats and sheep, marked by a high fever

135 to dose: to give medicine

136 to bleed: to take blood from a person or animal as a way of treating an illness (a method of treatment that was recognised as completely useless by the last quarter of the 19th century)

137 to besiege: to surround with the aim of attacking

138 shotgun: *Flinte*

139 seventeen-and-six: probably seventeen British pounds and six pence – A unified currency, the Australian pound, was not introduced until 1910.

140 hide: skin of an animal that is used for leather

141 crow [krəʊ]: large, black bird (*Krähe*)

142 eagle [ˈiːgl]: *Adler*

143 to have designs on s.o.: to be planning to achieve s.th., usually bad that should affect s.o.

mother!" and she rushes out and aims a broomstick[144] at the birds as though it were a gun, and says "Bung!" The crows leave in a hurry; they are cunning[145], but a woman's cunning[146] is greater.

Occasionally a bushman[147] in the horrors[148], or a villainous[149]-looking sundowner[150], comes and nearly scares the life out of her. She generally tells the suspicious[151]-looking stranger that her husband and two sons are at work below the dam, or over at the yard, for he always cunningly inquires for the boss.

Only last week a gallows-faced[152] swagman[153] – having satisfied himself that there were no men on the place – threw his swag down on the veranda, and demanded tucker[154]. She gave him something to eat; then he expressed his intention of staying for the night. It was sundown then. She got a batten[155] from the sofa, loosened the dog, and confronted the stranger, holding the batten in one hand and the dog's collar[156] with the other. "Now you go!" she said. He looked at her and at the dog, said "All right, mum," in a cringing[157] tone, and left. She was a determined-looking woman, and Alligator's yellow eyes glared[158] unpleasantly – besides, the dog's chawing[159]-up apparatus[160] greatly resembled that of the reptile he was named after.

She has few pleasures to think of as she sits here alone by the fire, on guard against a snake. All days are much the same to her; but on Sunday afternoon she dresses herself, tidies[161] the children, smartens up[162] baby,

---

[144] broomstick: *Besenstiel*
[145] cunning (adj.): clever in getting s.th. in a dishonest way
[146] cunning (noun): cleverness in getting s.th. in a dishonest way
[147] bushman (Australian English): a man who lives and wanders in the bush
[148] in the horrors (slang): mad, completely out of control often because of being drunk
[149] villainous [ˈvɪlənəs]: very evil
[150] sundowner (old-fashioned, Australian English): a tramp who seeks food and a place to sleep when it gets dark and knows he can't find work any more
[151] suspicious: *verdächtig*
[152] gallows-faced: looking like he has been hanged at the gallows (*Galgen*)
[153] swagman (colloquial, Australian English): formerly, a man travelling around looking for work and carrying his possessions in a swag (pack)
[154] tucker (old-fashioned, colloquial Australian English): food
[155] batten: long, narrow wooden board
[156] collar: *Kragen*
[157] cringing: showing fear
[158] to glare: to look at s.th./s.o. in an angry way
[159] to chaw: to chew
[160] chawing-up apparatus: i.e. mouth
[161] to tidy: to make s.o. look neat and clean
[162] to smarten up (colloquial): to make s.o. look neater and more attractive

and goes for a lonely walk along the bush track[163], pushing an old perambulator[164] in front of her. She does this every Sunday. She takes as much care to make herself and the children look smart[165] as she would if she were going to do the block[166] in the city. There is nothing to see, however, and not a soul to meet. You might walk for twenty miles along this track without being able to fix a point in your mind, unless you are a bushman. This is because of the everlasting[167], maddening sameness of the stunted trees – that monotony which makes a man long to break away and travel as far as trains can go, and sail as far as ships can sail – and farther.

But this bushwoman is used to the loneliness of it. As a girl-wife she hated it, but now she would feel strange away from it.

She is glad when her husband returns, but she does not gush[168] or make a fuss about[169] it. She gets him something good to eat, and tidies up the children.

She seems contented with her lot[170]. She loves her children, but has no time to show it. She seems harsh[171] to them. Her surroundings are not favourable[172] to the development of the "womanly" or sentimental side of [her] nature[173].

It must be near morning now; but the clock is in the dwelling house[174]. Her candle is nearly done; she forgot that she was out of candles. Some more wood must be got to keep the fire up, and so she shuts the dog inside and hurries round to the wood heap[175]. The rain has cleared off[176]. She seizes a stick, pulls it out, and – crash! the whole pile collapses.

---

[163] track: trail, path
[164] perambulator (formal): baby carriage, pram
[165] smart: clean and attractive
[166] to do the block (colloquial): to walk through the central parts of a city
[167] everlasting: never coming to an end
[168] to gush: to act or speak in a very excited and emotional way
[169] to make a fuss about s.th.: to overreact about s.th., to pay too much attention to s.th.
[170] lot: fate
[171] harsh: cruel, severe, unkind
[172] favourable: advantageous (*günstig*)
[173] nature: character
[174] dwelling house: the part of a house or the house you live in
[175] heap: pile
[176] to clear off: to move away

Yesterday she bargained with[177] a stray[178] blackfellow[179] to bring her some wood, and while he was at work she went in search of a missing cow. She was absent an hour or so, and the native black made good use of his time. On her return she was so astonished to see a good heap of wood by the chimney[180], that she gave him an extra fig[181] of tobacco, and praised him for not being lazy. He thanked her, and left with head erect[182] and chest well out. He was the last of his tribe[183] and a King[184]; but he had built that wood-heap hollow[185].

She is hurt now, and tears spring to her eyes as she sits down again by the table. She takes up a handkerchief to wipe the tears away, but pokes[186] her eyes with her bare[187] fingers instead. The handkerchief is full of holes, and she finds that she has put her thumb through one, and her forefinger[188] through another.

This makes her laugh, to the surprise of the dog. She has a keen[189], very keen, sense of the ridiculous[190]; and some time or other she will amuse bushmen with the story.

She had been amused before like that. One day she sat down "to have a good cry," as she said – and the old cat rubbed against her dress and "cried too." Then she had to laugh.

It must be near daylight now. The room is very close[191] and hot because of the fire. Alligator still watches the wall from time to time. Suddenly he becomes greatly interested; he draws[192] himself a few inches nearer the partition, and a thrill[193] runs through his body. The hair on the back of his neck begins to

---

177 to bargain with: to arrive at an agreement with s.o. about the price of s.th., to negotiate the price of s.th.
178 stray: happening to be wandering in the neighbourhood
179 blackfellow: Aborigine
180 chimney: *Schornstein*
181 fig: a very small amount
182 erect: upright in position, not bent down
183 tribe: *Stamm*
184 King: (here) chieftain of a tribe or clan
185 hollow: a wooden structure that holds a pile of wood
186 to poke: *stupfen*
187 bare: not covered by anything
188 forefinger: *Zeigefinger*
189 keen: sharp, highly developed
190 ridiculous: absurd
191 close: unpleasantly hot and stuffy because of a lack of fresh air
192 to draw oneself: to move in a certain direction
193 thrill: strong feeling of excitement

bristle[194], and the battle light[195] is in his yellow eyes. She knows what this means, and lays her hand on the stick. The lower end of one of the partition slabs has a large crack on both sides. An evil pair of small, bright bead[196]-like eyes glisten[197] at one of these holes. The snake – a black one – comes slowly out, about a foot[198], and moves its head up and down. The dog lies still, and the woman sits as one fascinated. The snake comes out a foot farther. She lifts her stick, and the reptile, as though suddenly aware of danger, sticks his head in through the crack on the other side of the slab, and hurries to get his tail round after him. Alligator springs, and his jaws[199] come together with a snap[200]. He misses, for his nose is large, and the snake's body close down in the angle[201] formed by the slabs and the floor. He snaps[202] again as the tail comes round. He has the snake now, and tugs it out[203] eighteen inches[204]. Thud[205], thud comes the woman's club on the ground. Alligator pulls again. Thud, thud. Alligator gives another pull and he has the snake out – a black brute[206], five feet long. The head rises to dart about[207], but the dog has the enemy close to the neck. He is a big, heavy dog, but quick as a terrier[208]. He shakes the snake as though he felt the original curse[209] in common with

---

[194] to bristle: to stand up on the back

[195] battle light: brightness in the eyes to indicate readiness to attack

[196] bead: a small, round piece of glass, wood, etc. with a hole in the middle through which a string is placed with other beads to make a necklace (*Halskette*)

[197] to glisten: to shine

[198] foot: one foot = 30.48 cm

[199] jaw: *Kiefer*

[200] with a snap: closing with a sudden movement, abruptly

[201] body close down in the angle (*Winkel*): i.e. there was hardly any distance between the snake's bent body and the slabs in the partition

[202] to snap: to bite s.th. bringing the jaws quickly together

[203] to tug out: to pull out with powerful movements

[204] inch: one inch = 2.54 cm

[205] thud: a sound like the one made when a heavy object hits s.th. else

[206] brute: beast

[207] to dart about: to move quickly and suddenly in many different directions

[208] terrier: small, active dog originally developed to hunt animals that live under the ground

[209] original curse (*Fluch*): a reference to the serpent (snake) in the Garden of Eden, which convinced Adam to eat the forbidden fruit of knowledge, thus bringing about the Fall of Man (*Sündenfall*) – The original curse can be considered to mean the same as *original sin* (*Erbsünde*). Cf. also **Genesis** 3:1–24 for the story of the expulsion from the Garden of Eden – In addition Gods tells the serpent that it shall be punished: the descendants of Adam and Eve "shall crush your head," (verse 15), and to Eve He says: "I will greatly increase your pains in childbearing; with pain you will give birth to children. Your desire will be for your husband, and he will rule over you." (verse 16)

mankind. The eldest boy wakes up, seizes his stick, and tries to get out of bed, but his mother forces him back with a grip[210] of iron. Thud, thud – the snake's back is broken in several places. Thud, thud – its head is crushed[211], and Alligator's nose skinned again.

She lifts the mangled[212] reptile on the point of her stick, carries it to the fire, and throws it in; then piles on[213] the wood and watches the snake burn. The boy and dog watch, too. She lays her hand on the dog's head, and all the fierce[214], angry light dies out of his yellow eyes. The younger children are quieted, and presently go to sleep. The dirty-legged boy stands for a moment in his shirt, watching the fire. Presently he looks up at her, sees the tears in her eyes, and, throwing his arms round her neck exclaims[215]:

"Mother, I won't never go drovin'[216]; blast me[217] if I do!"

And she hugs[218] him to her worn out[219] breast and kisses him; and they sit thus together while the sickly daylight breaks over the bush.

1. Compare and contrast the tone, diction, sentence structure, and plot of this short story with *How Muster-Master Stoneman Earned His Breakfast*. (Notice how sentences in this short story often begin with "she," and the frequent use of "and.")

2. What are the tense forms used in the narrative and explain their use?

3. What role does anthropomorphism (giving animals human characteristics) play in the story?

4. What might the snake/reptile be a symbol of?

5. Describe the role of women, men, and children in the story that the narrative seems to approve and disapprove of?

---

210 grip: grasp, the act of holding tightly
211 to crush: to press so as to break or injure
212 mangled: crushed and twisted so that s.th. is badly damaged
213 to pile on: to place a number of things in a pile (*Haufen*)
214 fierce: intense and aggressive
215 to exclaim: to say suddenly with great emotion
216 drovin': driving cattle or sheep
217 blast me (colloquial, BE): damn me
218 to hug: to put your arms around s.o. and hold this person tightly
219 worn out: very tired, exhausted

6. What role does the setting play?

7. How are Aborigines portrayed in the short story?

8. What parallels might you find with pioneers in the American West?

9. Explain the following:
   a) *Young Ladies' Journal*
   b) "Mother, I won't never go drovin'; blast me if I do!"
   c) ... sickly daylight breaks over the bush.

10. Compare this story with Rudyard Kipling's short story *Rikki-tikki-tavi*, in which a mongoose kills a cobra that is a threat to a family in India.

For further reading:

Henry Lawson. Selected Stories, A & R Classics, Sydney, 2001
The Penguin Henry Lawson, Short Stories, Penguin, Ringwood, Australia, 1986

The following films, though very commercial, reveal much about what the ideals of Australian masculinity and femininity are considered to be:

Crocodile Dundee, 1986
Australia, 2004

Katharine Susannah Prichard (1883–1969)

Katharine Susannah Prichard was born in Levuka, Fiji to Australian parents.

They later settled in Tasmania and Melbourne, where she attended South Melbourne College. She worked as a governess at a sheep station in New South Wales and later as a teacher in Melbourne. In 1908 Prichard made her first trip to London as a freelance[1] journalist for the *Melbourne Herald* and again in 1912 she left for England to pursue her career as a writer.

In 1916 she returned to Australia. After marrying Hugo Throssell in 1919 they settled in Western Australia. Prichard became active in both politics and writing. In 1920 she became a founding member of the Communist Party of Australia.

Among her many literary works her novels **Black Opal** (1921), which openly criticised capitalism, and **Coonardoo** (1929), a literary work, which for the first time suggested that an Aboriginal woman and a white Australian could have a loving relationship, are worthy of mention.

While visiting the Soviet Union in 1933, tragedy struck: Her husband, Hugo Throssell, shot himself when his business failed during the Great Depression. After the Second World War, she completed the goldfields trilogy, **The Roaring Nineties** (1946), **Golden Miles** (1948), and **Winged Seeds** (1950), that concentrated on social history in the context of the discovery and exploitation of gold in Western Australia.

Katharine Susannah Prichard died at her home in Greenmount, Western Australia in 1969.

Her writing career included thirteen novels, hundreds of articles, three published volumes of poems, numerous short stories, and a dozen plays.

To summarize her writing:

[1] freelance: *freiberuflich*

> Prichard's writing reveal[2] a commitment[3] not only to political purpose but to a liberal humanist tradition, stressing organic form, which held[4] that great art was beyond propagandist rhetoric. The message, in other words, must be both concealed[5] and revealed[6].

About the short story itself the author has written:

> [...] *Marlene* [...] [was] retrieved[7] from wanderings about the outback and country districts. *Marlene* is set in the southwest, near a coal-mining township. [...] [*Marlene* was] inspired by an intimate sympathy with men and women in the comedy and tragedy of their lives[8].

The short story was first published in *The Bulletin* in 1938.

---

[2] to reveal: to make s.th. known
[3] commitment: *Verpflichtung*
[4] to hold: to maintain (*behaupten*)
[5] to conceal: to hide
[6] in **The Penguin New Literary History of Australia**, Penguin Books, Ringwood, Australia, 1988, p. 379
[7] to retrieve: to find and bring back
[8] in **Happiness, Selected Short Stories by Katharine Susannah Prichard**, Angus and Robertson, Sydney, 1969, p. viii

MARLENE[9] (1938)

Coming out from the trees, the camp on the hillside was almost invisible. It crouched[10] among rocks and wet undergrowth[11], with the township[12] lying under mists[13] in the valley below. The wurlies[14] of bark[15], bagging[16] and matted[17] leaves had taken on the colouring of the rocks and tree trunks[18]. They were shaped like mounds[19] of earth: crude[20] shells[21] with open mouths. A breath of smoke betrayed them[22]. It hung in the air and drifted[23] away among the trees.

Two women riding along the bush track[24] detected[25] the first humpy[26], then another and another, until half a dozen were in sight about[27] a rough[28] open space. Dogs flew out, barking fiercely[29]. Two or three children, barelegged[30], lean[31], sallow[32], bright-eyed[33], with black tousled[34] hair, slid out from before the wurlies. A man lying beside a fire sat up and glanced at the women.

---

9 Marlene [mʌ'li:n]: name of German origin for "Mary" or "Miriam" (meaning "wished for child")
10 to crouch [kraʊtʃ] (fig.): to sit close to the ground
11 undergrowth: bushes and plants growing close to the ground
12 township: small town
13 mists: thin fog lying above the ground
14 wurlies (Aboriginal): huts of bags and brushwood
15 bark: *Rinde*
16 bagging: rough cloth from the bags
17 matted: packed down to form a dense mass
18 trunk: *Stamm*
19 mound: heap, pile
20 crude: rough, not carefully made
21 shell: *Schale*
22 betrayed them: (here): revealed, disclosed (*verriet*) where they were
23 to drift: to be carried along
24 track: path, trail
25 to detect: to discover the existence of s.th.
26 humpy (Aboriginal): a small, temporary shelter made from bark and tree branches with a tree usually used as the main support
27 about: round
28 rough [rʌf]: not smooth, not well taken care of
29 fiercely: aggressively, violently
30 barelegged: with no shoes
31 lean [li:n]: thin
32 sallow: rather pale in a way that seems to be unhealthy
33 bright-eyed: eager, fresh and enthusiastic
34 tousled ['taʊzld]: untidy

"Hullo, Benjy," the elderly woman on a grey horse called. "Sleeping in this morning? Where's Mollie?"

The man grunted[35], staring sullenly[36] over the rain-sodden[37] clearing[38]. Men and women appeared at the open mouths of other wurlies, all dressed as they had been sleeping, in faded[39] dungarees[40] and khaki[41] trousers, shirts and skirts grey with grime[42] and grease[43], threadbare[44] woollen jackets and coats – cast-off[45] clothing of the townspeople.

"Hullo, Mrs Boyd," some of the women called.

"This is Miss Cecily Allison," Mrs Boyd explained, introducing the girl on the chestnut[46] colt[47]. "Miss Allison's from England; going to write a book about the Aborigines. She wanted to see your camp."

"We're half-castes[48] here – not abos[49]," a morose[50], middle-aged man replied.

"And not 'at home' so early in the day," one of the young men added sarcastically. "It's a hell of a place to see, anyhow."

"Y're fergettin' y'r[51] manners, Albert – swearin'[52] before ladies!" one of the women said.

She giggled[53] shyly[54].

---

[35] to grunt: to make a low, short sound in your throat to show you are annoyed or uninterested

[36] sullenly: in a way showing you do not wish to speak because of being in a bad mood

[37] sodden: extremely wet, soaked

[38] clearing: open space

[39] faded: with the colour less bright because of being washed so often or because of being old and worn

[40] dungarees [ˌdʌŋgəˈriːz]: overalls made of jeans material (*Latzhose*)

[41] khaki [ˈkɑːki]: yellow-brown, a color often used for military uniforms

[42] grime: a thick layer of dirt or soot

[43] grease: thick, fatty oil

[44] threadbare: old and thin because of being used a lot

[45] cast-off: said of clothing that the original owner no longer wants to wear

[46] chestnut: reddish-brown

[47] colt: male horse or pony not older than four

[48] half-caste (negative): of white and Aborigine origin

[49] abo (colloquial, often negative): an Aborigine

[50] morose [məˈrəʊs]: bad-tempered, not talking much

[51] Y're fergettin' y'r (slang): You're forgetting your (manners).

[52] to swear: *Schimpfwörter benutzen*

[53] to giggle: to laugh in a silly way because of being amused, embarrassed or nervous

[54] shyly [ʃaɪli]: *schüchtern*

"How's yerself[55], Mrs Boyd?"

"I'm well, Tilly. But you're looking like drowned rats, the lot of you[56]. Why don't you shift[57] camp for the winter, George?"

Mrs Boyd sat her upstanding[58] mount[59] squarely[60], as well-conditioned as he[61] was. A good horsewoman, capable of managing her own affairs, it was evident. Her manner was authoritative, but kind and friendly.

"Where'd we shift to?" a fat, youngish woman asked jocosely[62]. Barefooted, she stood, a once-white dress dragged[63] across her heavy breast and thighs[64], a youngster slung[65] on one hip. A little laugh nibbled its way through[66] the crowd.

"This is the only place we're allowed to camp in the district[67],"the man who had first spoken said sourly[68]. "You know that, Mrs Boyd."

"The rain's been comin' down steady for two months." One of the other women raised a flat, uncomplaining treble[69].

"How on earth do you manage to get a dry spot in the humpies or keep your clothes dry?"

"We don't." The crowd laughed as though that were a good joke. "Our clothes are all soakin'[70]. There's not a dry blanket in the camp."

"We ought to be ducks. The rain'd run off our backs then."

"It's a disgrace[71] you should have to live like this," Mrs Boyd declared. "But what I came about this morning is Mollie. Where is she?"

---

[55] How's yerself (slang): How are you
[56] the lot of you: all of you
[57] to shift: to move from place to another
[58] upstanding: standing upright with the head up
[59] mount (formal, literary): horse you are riding
[60] sat squarely: sat on the saddle in a confident way in full control
[61] he: i.e. the male horse
[62] jocosely [ʤəˈkəʊsli] (formal): humorously
[63] to drag: to pull with force
[64] thigh [θaɪ]: *Hüfte*
[65] to sling, slung, slung: to place s.th. somewhere where it can hang loosely
[66] nibbled its way (fig.): managed to make itself heard – to nibble: to take small bites of s.th.
[67] district: *Gebiet, Bezirk*
[68] sourly [ˈsaʊəli]: bitterly
[69] to raise a treble: to begin to speak with a high voice
[70] soakin': completely wet
[71] disgrace: *Schande*

The crowd shifted uneasily. Eyes encountered[72] and glanced[73] aside. A wild crew[74] they looked in their shabby clothes, the women wearing remnants[75] of finery[76], a bright scarf or coloured cardigan over their draggled[77] dresses.

Brown-eyed, black-haired, they all were, but their skin varied from sickly yellow to weathered bronze. The women were sallow and tawny[78], the men darker. On most of the faces, thick noses and full lips denoted[79] the Aboriginal strain[80]; a few others had sharp, neat[81] features[82], showing no trace[83] of Aboriginal origin except in their eyes.

"Where is Mollie?" Mrs Boyd demanded. "I've been letting Mr Edward drive her in to the pictures on Saturday nights when he goes into town himself. But she didn't come back with him last week. He waited an hour for her."

"She's fair mad[84] about the pictures, Mollie," Ruby burbled[85].

"That's all very well, but it's not very considerate[86] of her to run away like this. She knows how busy we are just now with all the cows coming in. Mr Phillip and Mr Edward've got their hands full. I had to ride in with the mail myself this morning. And Mollie was very useful, helping with the milking and feeding poddies[87]."

"She's a fine kid, Mollie," Albert declared.

"But where is she? What's the matter?"

---

72 to encounter: to meet
73 to glance: to look quickly
74 crew [kru:]: (here): lot, group
75 remnants (plural): parts that remain of s.th. after being used
76 finery: elegant clothing
77 draggled: wet and dirty
78 tawny: brownish-yellow
79 to denote: to indicate
80 strain: descent, ancestry
81 neat: pleasing to look at, fine
82 feature: any part of the face such as the mouth, nose, etc.
83 trace: *Spur*
84 fair mad (colloquial): rather enthusiastic
85 to burble: to speak in a confused way that is difficult to understand
86 considerate: thoughtful (*rücksichtsvoll*)
87 poddy (Australian English): a handfed lamb or calf

The crowd surged[88]. Obviously, the question was disturbing[89]: it had to be evaded[90]. Exclamations[91] and suggestions clattered[92]. There was no surprise, no consternation[93], although everybody seemed upset, a little nervous and amused at Mrs Boyd's query[94].

Mrs Boyd guessed they were hiding Mollie. The child had got a quirk[95] about something: one of those mysterious urges[96] to go bush[97] with her own kind[98].

"Did y'know[99] Bill Bibblemun took bad[100] with the p'monia[101] and died in hospital, Sunday week?" somebody asked.

Others joined in eagerly.

"It was a grand funeral[102], Mrs Boyd."

"The Salvation Army[103] captain said Bill'd go straight to glory because he was a good Christian."

"He was, too. Testified[104] at street meetings and sang hymns – even when he was drunk."

"They said some beautiful prayers."

"All about his bein' washed in the blood of the lamb and his sins bein' whiter than snow."

"And the kids have all had measles[105]," Ruby boasted[106].

---

[88] to surge: to move quickly and with force in a certain direction
[89] disturbing: upsetting
[90] to evade: to avoid dealing with or talking about s.th.
[91] exclamation: sudden word or phrase spoken with emotion
[92] to clatter : to talk loudly and quickly
[93] consternation: feeling of anxiety or confusion, dismay
[94] query [ˈkwɪəri] (formal): question
[95] quirk: aspect of a person's behaviour that is strange
[96] urge: strong desire
[97] to go bush (colloquial, Australian English): to return to a primitive life in the bush
[98] kind: people of the same race or background
[99] y'know: you know
[100] to take bad (colloquial): to become ill
[101] p'monia: pneumonia [nju:ˈməʊni:ə]: a serious illness of the lungs
[102] funeral [ˈfju:nərəl]: ceremony for burying a dead person
[103] Salvation Army: *Heilsarmee*
[104] to testify: (here): to make a statement that you have been converted to Christianity and believe you are saved
[105] measles: *Masern*
[106] to boast: *prahlen*

"What's happened to Wally Williams?" Mrs Boyd inquired[107], willing to humour them. "He was to come over and cut fencing posts[108] for me last month."

There was a lull[109] in the rattle of voices[110], eyelids fell, wary[111] glances slid[112] under them. Coughing[113], a hoarse[114] whispering, filled the pause.

"He's gone up-country[115]," George said.

"You mean, he's in jail. What's he been up to now?"

"Well, you see, Mrs Boyd, it wasn't hardly Wally's fault," Tilly Lewis explained. "Jo Wiggins said some steers[116] had got out of his holding-paddocks[117], and he offered Wally two bob[118] for every steer he could track[119] and bring in. Wally took in a couple of cleanskins[120]. He thought they were Mr Wiggins's steers, natcherly[121] – "

"Naturally – at two bob apiece," Mrs Boyd agreed.

"But when the mounted trooper[122] found a couple of red poley[123] steer skins in Jo Wiggins's slaughteryard, Mr Wiggins put the blame on[124] to Wally – and Wally got two years[125]."

"Everybody knows Jo Wiggins's game," Mrs Boyd admitted[126]. "But Wally ought to keep his hands off cleanskins."

---

107 to inquire (formal): to ask
108 post: *Pfosten*
109 lull: a quiet period between times of activity
110 rattle of voices: (here): mixture of loud voices
111 wary ['weəri]: cautious
112 to slide, slid, slid: to move quietly and quickly
113 to cough [kɒf]: *husten*
114 hoarse [hɔːs]: sounding rough and unpleasant
115 up-country: to an area far from nearby towns
116 steer: castrated bull, i.e. ox kept for its meat
117 holding-paddock (Australian and New Zealand English): any area of fenced land to hold animals
118 bob: shilling, a former British and Australian coin, worth 1/20 of a pound
119 to track: to hunt down
120 cleanskin (Australian English): an unbranded animal
121 natcherly (slang): naturally
122 mounted trooper (USA and Australia): policeman on horseback
123 poley (Australian English): hornless cattle or cattle with their horns cut off
124 to put the blame on s.o. (normally without "to"): to maintain that s.o. is responsible for s.th. bad that happened
125 two years: i.e. two years in jail
126 to admit: *zugeben*

"Oh, he's not like that, Wally, Mrs Boyd. He's a real good stockman[127]. But if he can't get a job, he doesn't know what to do with hisself[128]. He's jest[129] got to be workin' cattle – "

"I know." Mrs Boyd laughed good-humouredly. "I suspect[130] he's 'worked'[131] calves from our back hills before now. We had an epidemic[132] of milkers[133] coming in without calves last year."

"If a cow drops[134] a calf in the bush, Mrs Boyd, the dingoes[135] are as likely to get it as – "

"Wally! Of course. But my money's on Wally[136]. I reckon[137] Jo Wiggins has had more of our calves than the dingoes."

Her horse, cropping[138] the young grass, swung[139] Mrs Boyd sideways. She saw the figure of a man sleeping before a smouldering[140] fire at the entrance of his shack[141]. Steam was rising from the damp[142] blanket that covered him.

"Who's that? "she asked.

"It's Charley," a woman who had been coughing incessantly[143] said. "He's not well".

"Better put that bottle away then," Mrs Boyd advised. "If the trooper comes round somebody'll be getting into trouble for selling Charley plonk[144] again. Where does he get the money to buy drink, anyhow?"

"The shopkeepers take his drawings for showcards[145] sometimes."

---

127 stockman: a man responsible for the care of livestock, especially cattle
128 hisself (slang): himself
129 jest: just
130 to suspect: to think that s.th. bad is likely to be true
131 worked: (here): stolen
132 epidemic: (here): a sudden increase in s.th. bad happening
133 milker: a cow that produces milk
134 to drop (colloquial): to give birth to
135 dingo: wild dog of Australia, much like a wolf
136 my money's on Wally: i.e. I think it's more likely that Wally got the calves than the dingoes did.
137 to reckon (informal): to think or suppose, to be of the opinion
138 to crop: to bite off and eat the top of grass
139 to swing, swung, swung: to cause to move in a curve
140 smouldering: burning slowly with hardly a flame
141 shack: primitive, small building made of wood and metal
142 damp: *feucht*
143 incessantly: constantly
144 plonk (BE): poor quality, cheap wine
145 for showcards: to use as a show bill, an advertising poster

"He's quite an artist in his own way, Charley," Mrs Boyd explained to her companion. "Self-taught. Could you show Miss Allison some of Charley's drawings, Lizzie?"

Charley's wife slipped away[146], burrowed into[147] the wurley, and returned with a black exercise book in her hands. Miss Allison dismounted[148] to look at the drawings, crude[149] outlines[150] of people and animals, a football match, the finish of a race.

Pleasure in Charley's drawings, awed[151] interest and expectancy animated his friends and relations.

"Well" – Mrs Boyd yanked[152] her horse's head round and straightened her back, smiling but implacable[153] – "have you made up your minds yet to tell me about Mollie?"

The faces about her changed. There was a moment of sombre[154], unresponsive silence.

Then Tilly Lewis exclaimed delightedly[155]: "Why, it's Mrs Jackson! She's been bad with the rheumatics[156]; but got up – and put on her hat for the visitors!"

A withered[157] little woman, a neat black hat perched[158] on her head, walked across the clearing, wearing a dingy[159] black dress and frayed[160] grey cardigan with an air of forlorn[161] propriety[162].

"Good morning, Myrtle," Mrs Boyd said. "I'm sorry to hear you've been having rheumatism."

---

146 to slip away: to leave quickly and quietly
147 to burrow into: (here): to go into a small and dark place to search for s.th.
148 to dismount: to get off a horse
149 crude: not skilled, simply made
150 outline: *Umriss*
151 awed [ɔ:d]: feeling overwhelming wonder, respect and admiration
152 to yank: to pull hard and quickly
153 implacable [ɪmˈplækəbl̩]: unwilling to make change one's opinion or take another course of action (*unnachgiebig*)
154 sombre [ˈsɒmbəʳ]: sad, melancholy
155 delightedly: in a way that shows you are extremely pleased
156 rheumatics (colloquial): rheumatism [ˈru:mətɪzəm]
157 withered: (here): looking very old because of being thin and having very dry skin
158 perched: (here): resting on
159 dingy [ˈdɪndʒi]: with the colour no longer bright and dirty
160 frayed [freɪd]: worn and starting to come apart
161 forlorn: lonely, miserable, unhappy
162 propriety [prəˈpraɪəti]: conformity to what is socially acceptable in conduct (*Verhalten*) or speech

"What can you expect, Miss Ann[163]?" The half-caste[164] held herself with some dignity[165]: her faded[166] eyes, ringed like agates[167], looked up at the pleasantly smiling, healthy, fresh-complexioned[168] woman on the big horse. "I'm not used to living out of doors."

"No, of course not," Mrs Boyd replied.

"You know I was brought up at the mission station[169]. And I've worked in some of the best homes in the district; but now – you wouldn't keep a sow[170] in the place where I've got to live."

"It's not right, Mrs Boyd," George muttered[171].

"No, it's not right," Mrs Boyd agreed. "But what can I do about it? Would you go into the Old Women's Home if I could get you in, Myrtle?"

"I've been there. The police took me from the hospital after I had rheumatic fever[172]. But I ran away – "

"She did, Mrs Boyd!" eager[173] voices chimed[174].

"She walked near on[175] a hundred and thirty miles[176] till she got here."

"Cooped up[177] in the city – with a lot of low-down[178] old women treatin' me like dirt. I've always kept myself to myself. I've always been respectable, Miss Ann."

---

163 Miss Ann: (here): A respectful way of addressing a female person in authority that was also used by Blacks in the South (USA).
164 half-caste (negative): a person whose parents are of different races
165 dignity: *Würde*
166 faded: no longer bright
167 agate ['ægət]: a hard stone with bands of different colours used for jewellery
168 fresh-complexioned: with the skin on one's face looking very healthy
169 mission station: school run by a religious organisation – Mrs Jackson is referring to the government policy of forcibly removing half-caste children from their parents. These children are known as the Stolen Generation, and were educated in church missions to later work as domestic servants in white families. Lasting from 1869 to 1969, this policy is now seen by most Australians as immoral.
170 sow [səʊ]: female pig
171 to mutter: to speak in a quiet way that is difficult to understand
172 rheumatic [ru'mætɪk] fever: a disease with the symptoms of a sore throat, fever, and pain in the joints (*Gelenke*)
173 eager: excited
174 to chime: (here): to agree
175 near on (colloquial): almost, nearly
176 mile: one mile = 1,609 km
177 cooped up: like an animal in a small cage
178 low-down: mean (*gemein*)

"Oh, yes, she's terrible respectable, Mrs Boyd," the chorus[179] went up[180].

"Nobody can't say Mrs Jackson isn't respectable!"

"All I want's to die in my own place – like any respectable person. It *is* my own place, Miss Ann, the house your father gave Tom and me; and Mr Henry had no right to turn us out[181]."

"She's breaking her heart, like any old abo, for the hunting grounds of her people," Albert said cynically. "They always want to go home to die, but, being half-and-half, it's a roof over her head Mrs Jackson wants, and a bed to lie on."

"I'll see what I can do about it, Myrtle," Mrs Boyd promised.

"Funny, isn't it?" Albert's lounging[182], graceful[183] figure tilted[184] back as he gazed at[185] her. "You're the granddaughter of one of the early settlers who shot off more blacks than any other man in the country. Mrs Jackson is the granddaughter of one of the few survivors, and related to the best families in the district. But you've got the land and the law on your side. They put the dogs onto her if she goes round the homesteads[186] asking for a bit of tucker[187] or old clothes.

"And this is the only spot where we're allowed to camp in the district."

"Something will have to be done about it," Mrs Boyd declared.

"What?" Albert demanded. "All the land about[188] has been taken up. It's private property now. We're not allowed to work in the mines. We're not allowed to sell the fish we catch – not allowed to shoot or trap[189]. They don't want us on the farms. They won't let us work on the roads. All we're allowed to do is draw rations[190] and rot[191] ... though there is some talk of packing us off to one of those damned reservations 'where

---

179 chorus: (here): the voices, all at the same time
180 went up: (here): said with loud voices
181 to turn s.o. out: to force s.o. to leave a place
182 to lounge [laʊndʒ]: to sit, lie, or stand in a lazy way
183 graceful: characterised by beauty of movement or form
184 to tilt: to bend with the upper part of s.th. becoming lower
185 to gaze at: to look steadily at s.o.
186 homestead (Australia): sheep or cattle station
187 tucker (collquial, Australian English): food
188 about: around here
189 to trap: to catch an animal in a trap (*Falle*)
190 to draw rations: to obtain rations (a fixed amount of food given regularly to s.o.)
191 to rot (fig.): *verrotten*

the diseased and dying remnants[192] of the native race are permitted to end their days in peace'. Excuse me quoting the local rag[193]."

"You can't say I haven't tried to help you," Mrs Boyd protested. "I've always given you work on my farm when I could."

A wry[194] smile twisted[195] the young man's mouth. "And paid us less than half you'd have had to pay other workers."

"Albert!" one of the women objected[196]. "Don't take any notice of him, Mrs Boyd."

"You're talking like one of those crazy agitators, Albert," Mrs Boyd cried hotly. "If you're not careful you'll find yourself being moved on."

"I'll remember you said so, Mrs Boyd." Albert grinned maliciously[197].

"It's hard on Albert not being able to get work, Mrs Boyd," Ruby expostulated[198]. "He's real clever: can read and write as good as any white man. When he went to school he could beat any of the boys."

"Lot of good it's ever done me," Albert sneered[199]. "If I'd been a myall[200] I'd've had a better life. The blacks of any tribe[201] share all they've got with each other. The whites grab[202] all they can for themselves – and let even their own relations starve."

"Do the Aboriginals treat half-castes better?" Miss Allison's voice rose clear and chilly[203] against his wrath[204].

"They don't treat us like vermin[205]." Albert might have been admiring[206] the gleam[207] of her hair or the horse she was holding. "Up in the nor'-west[208], when I was a kid, I went around with my mother's tribe. Never knew I was any different from the rest. Then my father got interested in

---

192 remnants: (here): people still left, survivors
193 rag (colloquial): worthless newspaper
194 wry [raɪ]: sarcastic, ironic
195 to twist: to cause to form an unusual shape
196 to object: to say that you disagree or are opposed to what was said or done
197 maliciously [məˈlɪʃəsli]: in a way showing hatred and a desire to harm s.o.
198 to expostulate [ɪkˈspɒstʃəleɪt] (formal): to argue with s.o. to try to change this person's opinion
199 to sneer: to smile in way that shows you have no respect for s.o.
200 myall [ˈmaɪəl] (Aboriginal): Aborigine living independently of society
201 tribe: *Stamm*
202 to grab: to seize, to take suddenly and roughly
203 chilly: uncomfortably cold
204 wrath [rɒθ]: extreme anger
205 vermin (fig.): animals like fleas or rats that are harmful and difficult to control
206 to admire: *bewundern*
207 gleam: shininess
208 nor'-west: northwest

me. Sent me down here to school. He died – and I've been trying to get a job ever since."

"Do you want to go back to your own people?"

Albert's anger resurged[209]. "My own people!" he jeered[210]. "Who are they? My father was as fair[211] as you are. I couldn't live in a blacks' camp now – though this is as bad. But I don't belong there. I think differently. We all do. We like soap and clean clothes when we can get them, and books. We want to go to the pictures and football matches. I want to work and have a house to live in, a wife and kids. But this is all I've got. These are my only people – mongrels[212] like myself."

"You shouldn't talk bitter like that, Albert," Mrs Jackson reproved[213]. "It does no good."

"Nothing does any good." He flung away[214] from the crowd and stalked off[215] behind the wurlies.

"He's sore[216] because he can't get work and the Protector[217] won't let Penny Carnarvon marry him," Ruby said. "Penny's in service[218], and she's such a good servant they don't want to lose her. But she's fond[219] of Albert. She says she'll learn[220] the Protector."

"She will, too."

"Stella did, didn't she?"

"Too right, she did."[221]

"She dropped a trayload[222] of dishes to get herself the sack[223] because she wanted to marry Bob. But the missus[224] forgave her and took it out of her

---

209 to resurge: to rise again
210 to jeer: to cry out with mockery
211 fair: light in colour
212 mongrel (fig.): dog that is a mixture of breeds
213 to reprove (formal): to tell s.o. you do not approve of what this person has said or done
214 to fling, flung, flung away: (here): to move away suddenly
215 to stalk off: to walk away in an angry and proud way
216 sore: upset and angry because you feel you have been treated unfairly
217 Protector: Protector of Aborigines (1838–1970s), a government official in charge of protecting the rights of Aborigines and preventing acts of injustice – They often controlled the social life of Aborigines, e.g. saying who they could or could not marry.
218 in service (old-fashioned): a servant
219 to be fond of: have a liking for s.o.
220 to learn s.o. (slang): to get s.o. to change his/her mind
221 Too right, she did. (colloquial): Yes, indeed.
222 trayload: what a tray (*Servierbrett*) can hold
223 to get yourself the sack (BE, colloquial): to be fired
224 missus (colloquial): mistress, i.e. a woman in a position of authority

wages[225]. Stella had to get herself in the family way[226], and make up to[227] the boss, before the Protector decided she'd better marry Bob."

"Penny'll be going for a little holiday soon, Albert says. Then perhaps they can get married and go up north. He's almost sure he can get a job on one of the stations."

"But where's Mollie?" Mrs Boyd returned to the attack. The crowd closed down on their laughter and gossip[228]. There was a disconcerted[229] shuffling[230] and searching for something to say.

"Mollie?"

"Yes, Mollie. It's no use pretending[231] you don't know where she is. If she's hiding, doesn't want to come home, I'm not going to worry about her. But I'll have to let the Department[232] know – "

"Hullo, Mrs Boyd!" A girl in a pink cotton frock[233] stood in the opening of a wurley behind the horses. A pretty little thing, sturdy[234] and self-possessed[235], but rather pale, she stood there, a small bundle[236] wrapped in a dirty shawl[237] in her arms.

"Mollie," Mrs Boyd gasped[238]. "Have you been getting a baby?"

The girl nodded[239], smiling.

"But you're only a child," Mrs Boyd cried. "You're not sixteen."

"I was sixteen last month," Mollie replied calmly.

"It's scandalous," Mrs Boyd exclaimed indignantly[240]. "Who's the father?"

---

225 wages: *Löhne*
226 to get yourself in a family way (colloquial): to get pregnant
227 to make up to s.o.: to try get s.o. to be nice or friendly again after s.th. bad happened
228 gossip: *Tratsch*
229 disconcerted: anxious, embarrassed
230 shuffling: moving from one foot to another because of being embarrassed
231 to pretend: to behave in such a way that other people believe s.th. that is not true
232 the Department: A number of Australian states and territories had and still have a Department of Aboriginal Affairs. In the past it was the aim of these agencies to allow Aborigines to die out and to assimilate those of mixed blood. Today these government agencies are trying to repair the damage of the past.
233 frock (BE, old-fashioned): dress
234 sturdy: strong, healthy
235 self-possessed: calm and confident in a difficult situation
236 bundle: s.th. wrapped (to wrap: *einwickeln*) or tied together
237 shawl [ʃɔ:l]: a heavy piece of cloth worn by women around the neck or used to wrap a baby
238 to gasp: to take a quick deep breath with your mouth open because of being surprised
239 to nod: to move your head up and down to mean "yes"
240 indignantly: in an angry way because you think s.th. is wrong or unfair

Mollie's eyes smiled back at her. "I been going with two or three boys in town."

The little crowd before her quivered[241] to breathless excitement: a sigh[242], as of relief[243], and a titter[244] of suppressed[245] mirth[246] escaped[247].

"You ought to be ashamed of yourself," Mrs Boyd declared furiously. "You know, I thought better of you, Mollie. I thought you were different from the other girls. You've lived with me for so many years, and I trusted you to behave yourself."

"Don't be angry," Mollie said quietly. "I couldn't help it ... and I like the baby."

"When did it happen?"

"Last night."

Mrs Boyd stared at the girl. She looked a little wan[248], but quite well.

"Is she all right?" she asked the crone[249] who had come out of the hut behind Mollie. "Had I better get the doctor to come out and see her, or arrange for her to go into hospital?"

"I've never felt better in my life," Mollie said. "Aunty May can look after me."

"No need to bother," the old half-caste beside Mollie mumbled[250] soothingly[251]. "She hadn't a bad time. I'd have sent her to the hospital – but everything happened in such a hurry."

"Let me see the child," Mrs Boyd demanded: turned her horse and rode to Mollie.

"She's very little and red," Mollie apologized, tenderly[252] lifting the dirty shawl that covered the baby.

Mrs Boyd leaned down from her saddle. It was the ugliest scrap[253] of humanity she had ever seen; but there was something vaguely familiar[254]

---

241 to quiver: to shake slightly, to tremble
242 sigh [saɪ]: *Seufzer*
243 as of relief: seemingly because of a feeling of happiness because s.th. unpleasant is over
244 titter: laughing quietly
245 suppressed: prevented from developing
246 mirth: happiness, merriment
247 to escape: (here): to come out without intention
248 wan [wɒn]: looking pale and weak
249 crone (negative): old woman
250 to mumble: to speak with a quiet voice that is not easy to understand
251 soothingly: in a way making s.o. feel less worried and anxious
252 tenderly: gently, lovingly
253 scrap: bit, small piece, fragment
254 familiar: *vertraut*, *bekannt*

in its tiny[255] crumpled[256] face. Cicely Allison dragged[257] her horse over the grass to look at the baby, too.

"Ra-ther sweet, isn't she?" she murmured[258] mechanically. "What are you going to call her?"

Mollie drew the shawl over the baby's face again. "Marlene," she said happily. The rain descended[259] in a gusty[260] squall[261], driving the half castes into their wurlies, the horsewomen back among the trees. As they rode, the older woman sagged[262] in her saddle, curiously[263] aged and grim[264].

"The sooner they're cleaned out of the district the better," she said viciously[265]. "They're an immoral lot[266], these half-castes."

"What about the whites who are responsible for them?" the girl on the chestnut colt asked.

She wondered whether it was a tragedy or a comedy she had been witnessing[267]. These people might live like dogs in their rotten[268] wurlies, with the dark bush behind them and the prosperous[269] little township spread[270] at their feet; but their aspirations[271] were all towards the ways and ideas of the white race. The exotic film star[272], and that baby in this dump[273] of outcasts[274] – what an indictment[275]! Yet Miss Allison suspected[276] they had tried to spare[277] the

255 tiny: very small
256 crumpled: crushed into folds or wrinkles (*Falten*)
257 to drag: to pull with force
258 to murmur: to say in a soft voice that is difficult to understand
259 to descend: to move downwards
260 gusty: with a wind suddenly increasing in strength
261 squall [skwɔːl]: a storm with rain or snow and a strong wind
262 to sag: to sink, to no longer sit upright
263 curiously: strangely and unusually
264 grim: serious, somber (*grimmig*)
265 viciously [ˈvɪʃəsli]: full of hatred and anger
266 lot (BE, colloquial): group of people
267 to witness: to experience, to be at the place where s.th. happens
268 rotten: in a terrible state and becoming worse
269 prosperous: wealthy, flourishing
270 spread: open to view over a large area
271 aspiration: strong desire to achieve s.th.
272 the exotic film star: a reference to Marlene Dietrich (1901–1992)
273 dump (fig.): area where rubbish is taken to
274 outcast: person not accepted by society
275 indictment [ɪnˈdaɪtmənt]: *vernichtende Anklage*
276 to suspect: to have an idea that s.th. is true
277 to spare: (here): to not confront s.o. with s.th. unpleasant

baby's grandmother, with simple kindliness[278], knowing the truth behind Mollie's bravado[279]. Had they altogether succeeded?

The camp on the hillside was moved on before the end of the month.

Questions about the short story:

1. Compare and contrast the diction and style of this short story with the previous two.
2. What tense form is used in the narration? Explain.
3. From what point of view is the story told? Which characters seem to be the spokespersons of the author?
4. What role do the animals play? Compare with *The Drover's Wife*?
5. "The message, in other words, must be both concealed and revealed." Do you agree that the author has been successful in this respect?
6. What aspects of Marxist ideology can you find in the short story?
7. Compare the female characters in the short story. What means are used to characterise them.
8. Explain: "… but there was something vaguely familiar in its tiny crumpled face."
9. What do you learn about the history of the relationship between Aborigines and the colonisers up to 1938? Research what has happened after 1938 to the present time.
10. Imagine how the story might continue.
11. Compare the racism and injustice revealed in the short story with the situation of Blacks and Native Americans in the USA. Cf. **A Lesson Before Dying** and **Black Like Me** (both published by Diesterweg).

For further reading:

Happiness, Selected Short Stories by Katharine Susannah Prichard, Angus and Robertson, Sydney, 1967

The films **Australia** (2007) and **Rabbit-Proof Fence** (2002) both deal with the problem of The Stolen Generation.

---

[278] kindliness: being friendly and caring

[279] bravado [brəˈvaːdəʊ]: display of courage and self-confidence with the aim of impressing

Archie Weller (1957-)

Archie Weller, a writer with Aboriginal roots, was born in Perth, Western Australia. He grew up on an isolated farm and attended various Perth boarding schools, finishing his education at the Western Australian Institute of Technology with film and creative writing as the main subjects. He also worked in a variety of jobs, as a farm hand, printer, and gardener. He developed a love for literature and began writing at an early age. His first novel, **The Day of the Dog** (1981), portrays the tragic life of a part-Aborigine in the street culture of Perth. It was later made into a film (1991). With the publication of **Going Home** (1986) Archie Weller cemented his reputation as a writer of significance. It contains nine short stories and a novella that primarily deal with the Aboriginal youth culture of southwest Western Australia. The title story is included in this anthology. His other works include the plays *Sunset and the Shadows* (1989) and *Nidjera* (1990) the films *Tilt* (1978), *Chronicle of the Blue Elves* (1991), and *Journey of the Stone People* (1991).

Going Home (1986)
by Archie Weller

I want to go home.
I want to go home.
Oh, Lord, I want to go home[1].

Charlie Pride[2] moans[3] from a cassette, and his voice slips out[4] of the crack[5] the window makes. Out into the world of magpies'[6] soothing[7] carols[8], and parrots' cheeky[9] whistles, of descending[10] darkness and spirits[11].

The man doesn't know that world. His is the world of the sleek[12] new Kingswood[13] that speeds down the never-ending highway.

At last he can walk this earth with pride, as his ancestors did many years before him. He had his first exhibition of paintings a month ago. They sold well, and with the proceeds[14] he bought the car.

The slender[15] black hands swing[16] the shiny black wheel around a corner. Blackness forms a unison[17] of power.

For five years he has worked hard and saved and sacrificed[18]. Now, on his twenty-first birthday, he is going home.

New car, new clothes, new life.

---

1 from "Detroit City," a song originally made famous by the white country music singer Bobby Bare (1935 –) in 1963, cf. lyrics at the end of the story
2 Charlie Pride (1938 –): African-American country music singer
3 to moan: *stöhnen*
4 to slip out: to move out of s.th. quietly and quickly
5 crack: (here): small opening
6 magpie: *Elster*
7 soothing: making you less anxious and worried
8 carol: joyful hymn or religious song
9 cheeky (BE, colloquial): *frech*
10 descending: moving downwards
11 spirit: *Geist*
12 sleek: elegant
13 Kingswood: Holden Kingswood, car manufactured by General Motors in Australia from 1968 to 1984
14 proceeds: profits, money earned for s.th.
15 slender: thin in an attractive way
16 to swing, swung, swung: to move in a curve
17 unison: complete harmony, union
18 to sacrifice: to give up s.th. that is important or valuable to you in order to get s.th. that seems more important

He plucks[19] a cigarette from the packet beside him, and lights up.

His movements are elegant and delicate. His hair is well-groomed[20], and his clothes are clean.

Billy Woodward is coming home in all his might, in his shining armour[21].

Sixteen years old. Last year at school.

His little brother Carlton and his cousin Rennie Davis, down beside the river, on that last night before he went to the college in Perth[22], when all three had had a goodbye drink, with their girls beside them.

Frogs croaking[23] into the silent hot air and some animal blundering[24] in the bullrushes[25] on the other side of the gentle river. Moonlight on the ruffled[26] water. Nasal voices whispering and giggling[27]. The clink[28] of beer bottles.

That year at college, with all its schoolwork, and learning, and discipline, and uniformity, he stood out alone in the football carnival[29].

Black hands grab the ball. Black feet kick the ball. Black hopes go soaring[30] with the ball to the pasty[31] white sky.

No one can stop him now. He forgets about the river of his Dreaming[32] and the people of his blood and the girl in his heart.

The year when he was eighteen, he was picked by a top city team as a rover[33]. This was the year that he played for the state[34], where he was voted best and fairest[35] on the field.

---

[19] to pluck: to pull out
[20] well-groomed: neatly cut and combed
[21] armour: a metal suit formerly worn by knights (*Ritter*) in the middle ages – cf. the expression: "a knight in shining armour," i.e. a heroic champion
[22] Perth: large city in southwestern Australia and capital of Western Australia
[23] to croak: to make a rough, low sound like a frog
[24] to blunder: to stumble, to move about bumping into things or knocking them over
[25] bullrush: tall, grasslike plant found in marshes (land that is constantly wet)
[26] ruffled: with small waves, not smooth
[27] to giggle: to laugh in a silly way
[28] clink: sharp, ringing sound that glasses make when they hit together
[29] carnival (Australian English): sports meeting
[30] to soar (fig.): to rise quickly
[31] pasty: pale and unhealthy-looking
[32] river of his Dreaming: i.e. his origins in the context of Aboriginal cosmology – Dreaming is a term used to describe the Aboriginal concept of their history and origins that include mythical stories.
[33] rover (Australian football): a player that has no fixed position
[34] for the state: i.e. for the state college
[35] fairest: the most honest

That was a year to remember.

He never went out to the park[36] at Guildford[37], so he never saw his people: his dark, silent staring people, his rowdy[38], brawling[39], drunk people.

He was white now.

Once, in the middle of the night, one of his uncles had crept around to the house he rented and fallen asleep on the verandah. A dirty pitiful carcass[40], encased[41] in the black greatcoat[42] that had smelt of stale[43] drink and lonely, violent places. A withered[44] black hand had clutched[45] an almost-empty metho[46] bottle.

In the morning, Billy had shouted at the old man and pushed him down the steps, where he stumbled[47] and fell without pride. The old man had limped[48] out of the creaking[49] gate, not understanding.

The white neighbours, wakened by the noise, had peered[50] out of their windows at the staggering[51] old man stumbling down the street and the glowering[52] youth muttering[53] on the verandah. They had smirked[54] in self-righteous[55] knowledge.

Billy had moved on the next day.

---

[36] park: area of land provided by the government where Aborigines live
[37] Guildford: suburb of Perth
[38] rowdy: making a lot of noise and likely to cause trouble
[39] to brawl [brɔːl]: to take part in noisy fights
[40] carcass (fig.): dead animal
[41] to encase: to cover completely
[42] greatcoat: a long, heavy coat
[43] stale: no longer fresh
[44] withered: looking old and weak
[45] to clutch: to hold tightly
[46] metho (Australian English, colloquial): methylated spirits, a kind of alcohol that is sometimes drunk because of its cheapness, but is poisonous
[47] to stumble: to walk in an unsteady way
[48] to limp: to walk with an uneven step, especially when one leg is weak or injured
[49] creaking: making a sound that a door sometimes makes when you open it or a wooden floor when you step on it
[50] to peer: to look closely at s.th. that is difficult to see
[51] to stagger: to walk with unsteady steps as if you are about to fall
[52] to glower [ˈglaʊəʳ]: to look in an angry and aggressive way
[53] to mutter: to say in a quiet voice that is difficult to understand
[54] to smirk: to smile showing self-satisfaction and that you don't think much of another person
[55] self-righteous: feeling that you are always morally right and everyone else wrong

William Jacob Woodward passed fifth year with flying colours[56]. All the teachers were proud of him. He went to the West Australian Institute of Technology[57] to further his painting, to gain[58] fame that way as well.

He bought clean, bright clothes and cut off his long hair that all the camp[59] girls had loved.

Billy Woodward was a handsome youth, with the features of his white grandfather and the quietness of his Aboriginal forebears[60]. He stood tall and proud, with the sensitive lips of a dreamer and a faraway look in his serene[61] amber[62] eyes.

He went to the nightclubs regularly and lost his soul in the throbbing[63], writhing[64] electrical music as the white tribe[65] danced their corroboree[66] to the good life.

He would sit along at the darkened corner table, or with a painted-up white girl – but mostly alone. He would drink wine and look around the room at all the happy or desperate people.

He was walking home one night from a nightclub when a middle-aged Aboriginal woman stumbled out of a lane[67].

She grinned up at him like the Gorgon[68] and her hands clutched at[69] his body, like the lights from the nightclub.

"Billy! Ya[70] Billy Woodward, unna[71]?"

---

56 with flying colours (fig.): with very good marks

57 the West Australian Institute of Technology: in Perth, founded in 1966 was renamed the Curtin University of Technology in 1986

58 to gain: to acquire, to get

59 camp: town camp, an area with primitive housing outside towns where Aborigines were forced to live

60 forebear: ancestor

61 serene [sə'ri:n]: peaceful, calm

62 amber: yellowish-brown like the colour of amber (*Bernstein*)

63 to throb: to pulsate, to have a strong rhythmic beat

64 to writhe [raɪð]: to twist as if in pain

65 tribe: *Stamm*

66 corroboree [kə'rɒbəri:] (Dharuk, Aboriginal language of the Port Jackson area): (usually): a festivity with songs and symbolic dances at night by which Aborigines celebrate events of importance

67 lane: narrow road between houses, fences, hedges

68 Gorgon: any of three snake-haired sisters in Greek mythology whose appearance turns the beholder to stone

69 to clutch at: to suddenly take hold of s.th.

70 Ya (slang): You are

71 unna (slang): aren't you

"Yes. What of it?"[72] he snapped[73].

"Ya[74] dunno[75] me? I'm ya[76] Aunty Rose, from down[77] Koodup[78]."

She cackled[79] then. Ugly, oh, so ugly. Yellow and red eyes and broken teeth and a long, crooked, white scar[80] across her temple[81]. Dirty grey hair all awry[82].

His people.

His eyes clouded over in revulsion[83]. He shoved[84] her away and walked off quickly.

He remembered her face for many days afterwards whenever he tried to paint a picture. He felt ashamed to be related to a thing like that. He was bitter that she was of his blood.

That was his life: painting pictures and playing football and pretending. But his people knew. They always knew.

In his latest game of football he had a young part-Aboriginal opponent who stared at him the whole game with large, scornful[85] black eyes seeing right through him.

After the game, the boy's family picked him up in an old battered[86] station wagon[87].

Billy, surrounded by all his white friends, saw them from afar off. He saw the children kicking an old football about with yells[88] and shouts of laughter and two lanky[89] boys slumping against[90] the door yarning[91] to

---

[72] What of it?: *Was ist dabei?*
[73] to snap: (here): to say in an angry, impatient way
[74] ya (slang): you
[75] dunno (slang): don't know
[76] ya (slang): your
[77] from down: southward from
[78] Koodup: small town in Western Australia
[79] to cackle: to laugh in a loud and unpleasant way
[80] scar: *Narbe*
[81] temple: *Schläfe*
[82] awry [əˈraɪ]: untidy, disorderly
[83] in revulsion: with a feeling of disgust or horror
[84] to shove [ʃʌv]: to push in a rough way
[85] scornful: with open dislike and disrespect (*verächtlich*)
[86] battered: old, used a lot and therefore in a bad condition
[87] station wagon: *Kombiwagen*
[88] yell: loud cry of excitement
[89] lanky: ungracefully tall and thin
[90] to slump against: to lean against s.th. in a careless manner
[91] to yarn (informal): to speak for a long time about insignificant things

their hero, and a buxom[92] girl leaning out the window and an old couple[93] in the back. The three boys, glancing[94] up, spotted[95] debonair[96] Billy. Their smiles faded[97] for an instant and they speared[98] him with their proud black eyes.

So Billy was going home, because he had been reminded of home (with all its carefree joys) at that last match.

It's raining now. The shafts[99] slant down[100] from the sky, in the glare[101] of the headlights[102]. Night-time, when woodarchis[103] come out to kill, leaving no tracks[104]: as though they are cloud shadows passing over the sun.

Grotesque trees twist[105] in the half-light. Black tortured[106] figures, with shaggy[107] heads and pleading[108] arms. Ancestors crying for remembrance. Voices shriek[109] or whisper in tired chants[110]: tired from the countless warnings that have not been heeded[111].

They twirl around[112] the man, like the lights of the city he knows. But he cannot understand these trees. They drag[113] him onwards, even when he thinks of turning back and not going on to where he vowed[114] he would never go again.

A shape, immovable and impressive as the tree it is under, steps into the road on the Koodup turn-off[115].

---

92 buxom [ˈbʌksəm]: well-built, plump (*mollig*) but sexually attractive
93 couple: *Ehepaar*
94 to glance: to take a quick look at s.th. or s.o.
95 to spot: to notice suddenly
96 debonair [ˌdebɔˈneɔʳ]: refined, sophisticated (*flott*)
97 to fade: (here): to disappear gradually
98 to spear: to throw a spear (*Speer*) at s.o. or s.th.
99 shaft: narrow strip, ray, beam (*Strahl*)
100 to slant down: to move down at an angle, not straight down
101 glare: a very bright, unpleasant light
102 headlight: *Scheinwerfer*
103 woodarchis (Aboriginal language): evil spirits, small hairy men with red eyes
104 track: mark on the ground (*Spur*)
105 to twist: to bend or turn into a shape or position that is not normal or natural
106 tortured: suffering severely
107 shaggy: having long and untidy hair
108 to plead: to ask for s.th. in a very strong and earnest way
109 to shriek [ʃriːk]: to scream
110 chant: words or phrases that a group of people repeatedly shout or sing
111 to heed [hiːd]: to pay close attention to s.o. or s.th.
112 to twirl around: to move quickly around s.th. or s.o.
113 to drag: to pull s.th. or s.o. along with effort and difficulty
114 to vow [vaʊ]: to make a formal and serious promise to do s.th.
115 turn-off: a place where a road leads away from a more important or larger road

An Aboriginal man.

Billy slews[116] to a halt, or he will run the man over.

Door opens.

Wind and rain and coloured man get in.

"Ta[117], mate[118]. It's bloody[119] cold 'ere[120]," the coloured man grates[121], then stares quizzically[122] at Billy, with sharp black eyes. "Nyoongah[123], are ya[124], mate?"

"Yes."

The man sniffs[125] noisily, and rubs a sleeve[126] across his nose.

"Well, I'm Darcy Goodrich, at any rate[127], bud[128]."

He holds out a calloused[129] hand. Yellow-brown, blunt[130] scarred[131] fingers, dirty nails. A lifetime of sorrow[132] is held between the fingers.

Billy takes it limply[133].

I'm William Woodward.'

"Yeah[134]?" Fathomless[135] eyes scrutinise[136] him again from behind the scraggly[137] black hair that falls over his face.

"Ya goin' anywheres[138] near Koodup, William?"

"Yes."

---

116 to slew : to skid, to suddenly turn or slide in another direction

117 ta [tɑː] (BE, slang): thanks

118 mate (BE, informal): a friendly way of addressing a male stranger

119 bloody (BE, slang): very

120 'ere (informal): here

121 to grate: to speak with a harsh voice

122 quizzically: in a questioning way, with puzzlement

123 Nyoongah (Aboriginal language): (here): an Aboriginal from the southwest, or any part-Aboriginal person

124 ya (slang): you

125 to sniff: to breathe in and out with a lot of noise

126 sleeve: *Ärmel*

127 at any rate: *auf jeden Fall*

128 bud [bʌd] (informal, primarily AE, short form for "buddy"): mate, friend

129 calloused ['kæləst]: said of skin that is hard and rough because of hard work

130 blunt: (here): short and thick

131 scarred: *vernarbt*

132 sorrow ['sɒrəʊ]: feeling of sadness or grief because of an unhappy life

133 limply: not firmly, not energetically

134 yeah [jeə] (informal): Is that right?

135 fathomless: (here): seemingly without a bottom

136 to scrutinise: to examine s.th. or s.o. carefully

137 scraggly: untidy, irregular in growth

138 anywheres (informal): anywhere

"Goodoh[139]. This is a nice car ya got 'ere[140]. Ya must 'ave[141] plen'y[142] of boya[143], unna[144]?"

Silence from Billy.

He would rather not have this cold, wet man beside him, reminding him.

He keeps his amber eyes on the lines of the road as they flash[145] under his wheels.

White ... white ... white ...

"Ya got a smoke, William?"

"Certainly. Help yourself."

Black blunt fingers flick open[146] his expensive cigarette case.

"Ya want one too, koordah[147]?"

"Thanks."

"Ya wouldn't be Teddy Woodward's boy, would ya, William?"

"Yes, that's right. How are Mum and Dad – and everyone?"

Suddenly he has to know all about his family and becomes lost in their sea of brownness.

Darcy's craggy[148] face flickers at[149] him in surprise, then turns, impassive[150] again, to the rain-streaked[151] window. He puffs on[152] his cigarette quietly.

"What, ya don't know?" he says softly. "Ya Dad was drinkin' metho. 'E[153] was blind[154] drunk, an'[155] in the 'orrors[156], ya know? Well, this truck came out of nowhere when 'e was crossin' the road on a night like this. Never seen 'im[157]. Never stopped or nothin'. Ya brother Carl found 'im

139 goodoh (Australian English, informal): an exclamation of pleasure
140 'ere (informal): here
141 'ave (informal): have
142 plen'y (informal): plenty
143 boya (Aboriginal language): money
144 unna (slang): (here): mustn't you
145 to flash: to shine very brightly for a short time
146 to flick open: to open with a quick, sudden movement
147 koordah (Aboriginal language): friend, brother
148 craggy: rough and having many deep lines
149 to flicker at: (here): to suddenly move towards, showing emotion
150 impassive: not showing any feeling or emotion
151 rain-streaked: with long, thin marks of rain
152 to puff on: to quickly breathe in and exhale smoke from a cigarette
153 'E (informal): he
154 blind (informal): completely
155 an' (informal): and
156 in the 'orrors (informal): in the horrors: completely intoxicated (*berauscht*)
157 'im (informal): him

next day an' there was nothin' no one could do then. That was a couple of years back now."

Billy would have been nineteen then, at the peak[158] of his football triumph. On one of those bright white nights, when he had celebrated his victories with wine and white women, Billy's father had been wiped off the face[159] of his country – all alone.

He can remember his father as a small gentle man who was the best card cheat[160] in the camp. He could make boats out of duck feathers and he and Carlton and Billy had had races by the muddy[161] side of the waterhole[162], from where his people had come long ago, in the time of the beginning.

The lights of Koodup grin[163] at him as he swings[164] around a bend[165]. Pinpricks[166] of eyes, like a pack of foxes waiting for the blundering[167] black rabbit. "Tell ya what, buddy. Stop off at the hotel an' buy a carton[168] of stubbies[169]."

"All right, Darcy." Billy smiles and looks closely at the man for the first time. He desperately feels that he needs a friend as he goes back into the open mouth of his previous life. Darcy gives a gap-toothed[170] grin.

"Bet ya can't wait to see ya people again."

His people: ugly Aunty Rose, the metho-drinking Uncle, his dead forgotten father, his wild brother and cousin. Even this silent man. They are all his people.

He can never escape.

The car creeps in[171] beside the red brick[172] hotel.

The two Nyoongahs scurry[173] through the rain and shadows and into the glare of the small hotel bar.

---

[158] peak: height, most successful time
[159] to wipe off the face of s.th. (idiom): to completely destroy or remove
[160] card cheat: person who plays cards dishonestly
[161] muddy: *schlammig*
[162] waterhole: well (*Quelle*)
[163] to grin: *grinsen*
[164] to swing: (here): to move in a curve
[165] bend: curve in a road
[166] pinprick: very small hole as made by a pin
[167] to blunder: (here): to be careless and get caught
[168] carton: (here): a cardboard box that holds a number of bottles
[169] stubbie: a small bottle of beer with a square shape that is sold in Australia
[170] gap-toothed: with some of the teeth missing
[171] to creep in: (here): to slow down and stop
[172] brick: *Backstein*
[173] to scurry: to run with short, quick steps

The barman is a long time coming, although the bar is almost empty. Just a few old cockies[174] and young larrikins[175], right down the other end. Arrogant grey eyes stare at Billy. No feeling there at all.

"A carton of stubbies, please."

"Only if you bastards[176] drink it down at the camp. Constable[177] told me you mob[178] are drinking in town and just causing trouble."

"We'll drink where we bloody like, thanks, mate."

"Will you, you cheeky[179] bastard?" The barman looks at Billy, in surprise. "Well then, you're not gettin' nothin' from me. You can piss off[180], too, before I call the cops. They'll cool you down, you smart black bastard."

Something hits Billy deep inside with such a force that it makes him want to clutch hold of the bar[181] and spew up[182] all his pride.

He is black and the barman is white, and nothing can ever change that.

All the time he had gulped in[183] the wine and joy of the nightclubs and worn neat[184] fashionable clothes and had white women admiring him, played the white man's game with more skill than most of the wadgulas[185] and painted his country in white man colours to be gabbled[186] over by the wadgulas: all this time he has ignored his mumbling[187], stumbling tribe and thought he was someone better.

Yet when it comes down to it all[188], he is just a black man.

Darcy sidles up[189] to the fuming[190] barman.

---

174 cocky (Australian English, informal): farmer
175 larrikin (Australian English, slang): mischievous person who refuses to accept authority and norms of behaviour and is always enjoying himself
176 bastard: miserable, disagreeable person
177 constable: local policeman
178 mob (Australian English): group of people, lot
179 cheeky (BE, informal): rude, disrespectful
180 to piss off (BE, slang): to go away, to leave
181 bar: long, wide table on which drinks are served
182 to spew up (BE, informal): to vomit, to cause the food in your stomach to go back through your mouth
183 to gulp in: to drink quickly
184 neat: pleasing, admirable
185 wadgulas (Aboriginal language): white people
186 to gabble over (informal): to talk about s.th. or s.o. quickly and in a way difficult to understand
187 to mumble: to speak in a quiet voice that is not clear
188 when it comes down to it all: *letzten Endes*
189 to sidle up: to move along sideways
190 fuming: extremely angry

" 'Scuse[191] me, Mr 'Owett[192], but William 'ere just come 'ome[193], see," he whines[194] like a beaten dog. "We *will* be drinkin' in the camp, ya[195] know."

"Just come home, eh? What was he inside[196] for?"

Billy bites his reply back so it stays in his stomach, hard and hurtful as a gallstone[197].

"Well all right, Darcy. I'll forget about it this time. Just keep your friend out of my hair."

Good dog, Darcy. Have a bone, Darcy. Or will a carton of stubbies do?

Out into the rain again.

They drive away and then turn down a track[198] about a kilometre out of town.

Darcy tears off a bottle top, handing the bottle to Billy. He grins.

"Act stupid, buddy, an' ya go a lo – ong way in this town."

Billy takes a long draught[199] of the bitter gold liquid. It pours down his throat and into his mind like a shaft of amber sunlight after a gale[200]. He lets his anger subside[201].

"What ya reckon[202], Darcy? I'm twenty-one today."

Darcy thrusts out[203] a hand, beaming[204].

"Tw'n'y[205]-bloody-one, eh?[206] 'Ow's[207] it feel?"

"No different from yesterday."

Billy clasps[208] the offered hand firmly.

---

191 'scuse (informal): excuse
192 'Owett: Howett
193 William 'ere just come 'ome: William here has just come home
194 to whine: to make a long, high, unpleasant sound because of being in pain or unhappy
195 ya (slang): you
196 inside (informal): in jail
197 gallstone: *Gallenstein*
198 track: rough path or road
199 draught [drɑːft]: the act of drinking a certain amount of liquid
200 gale: strong wind
201 to subside: to become quieter or calmer
202 to reckon (BE, informal): to have an opinion of s.th.
203 to thrust out: to move suddenly in a certain direction
204 beaming: with a wide and happy smile
205 tw'n'y (informal): twenty
206 eh? (informal): *Was?*
207 'ow's (informal): How does
208 to clasp: to hold s.th. tightly

They laugh and clink[209] bottles together in a toast[210], just as they reach the camp.

Dark and wet, with a howling[211] wind. Rain beating upon the shapeless humpies[212]. Trees thrash[213] around the circle of the clearing[214] in a violent rhythm of sorrow and anger, like great monsters dancing around a carcass[215].

Darcy indicates a hut clinging to[216] the edge of the clearing.

"That's where ya mum lives."

A rickety[217] shape of nailed-down tin[218] and sheets of iron. Two oatbags[219], sewn[220] together, form a door. Floundering[221] in a sea of tins[222] and rags[223] and parts of toys or cars. Mud everywhere.

Billy pulls up[224] as close to the door as he can get. He had forgotten what his house really looked like.

"Come on, koordah. Come an' see ya ole mum. Ya might be lucky, too, an' catch ya brother."

Billy can't say anything. He gets slowly out of the car while the dereliction[225] looms up[226] around him.

The rain pricks at[227] him, feeling him over[228].

He is one of the brotherhood.

---

[209] to clink: to make a sharp, ringing sound as when two bottles or glasses hit each other
[210] toast: act of wishing s.o. happiness
[211] to howl: to make a long, loud noise
[212] humpy: hut used by Aborigines
[213] to thrash: to move in a violent or uncontrollable way
[214] clearing: open space where there are no trees
[215] carcass: dead body of an animal
[216] to cling to (fig.): to hold tightly to s.th. or s.o.
[217] rickety: not strong or well made, likely to break
[218] tin: *Blech*
[219] oatbag: bag to hold oats (*Hafer*)
[220] to sew, sewed, sewn [səʊ]: *nähen*
[221] to flounder (fig.): to move with difficulty in water or mud (*Schlamm*)
[222] tin: *Dose*
[223] rag: piece of torn, old cloth
[224] to pull up: to stop
[225] dereliction (formal): state of being in a bad condition because of not being properly cared for
[226] to loom up: to appear as a large shape that is threatening
[227] to prick at: to cause small, sharp feelings of pain
[228] to feel over: to touch everywhere

A mouth organ's[229] reedy[230] notes slip in and out between the rain. It is at once a profoundly[231] sorrowful yet carefree tune that goes on and on.

Billy's fanfare[232] home.

He follows Darcy, ducking[233] under the bag door. He feels unsure and out of place and terribly alone.

There are six people: two old women, an ancient man, two youths and a young, shy, pregnant woman.

The youth nearest the door glances up with a blank[234] yellowish face, suspicion[235] embedded[236] deep in his black eyes. His long black hair that falls over his shoulders in gentle curls[237] is kept from his face by a red calico[238] headband. Red for the desert sands whence[239] his ancestors came, red for the blood spilt[240] by his ancestors when the white tribe came. Red, the only bright thing in these drab[241] surroundings.

The youth gives a faint[242] smile at Darcy and the beer.

"G'day[243], Darcy. Siddown[244] 'ere. 'Oo ya mate is? [245]"

"Oo'd ya think[246], Carl, ya dopy[247] prick[248]? 'E's ya brother come 'ome[249]."

Carlton stares at Billy incredulously[250], then his smile widens a little and he stands up, extending[251] a slim[252] hand.

---

229 mouth organ: harmonica
230 reedy: shrill
231 profoundly: deeply
232 fanfare ['fænfeəʳ]
233 to duck: to move your head or body to avoid s.th.
234 blank: expressionless
235 suspicion [sə'spɪʃən]: distrust (*Misstrauen*)
236 embedded: fixed firmly
237 gentle curls: *weiche Locken*
238 calico ['kælɪkəʊ]: heavy cotton
239 whence (old-fashioned): from where
240 to spill, spilt, spilt: *vergießen*
241 drab: dull, not bright
242 faint [feɪnt]: weak, slight
243 g'day (Australian English): good day, hello
244 siddown (informal): sit down
245 'Oo ya mate is? (informal): Who is your mate?
246 Oo'd ya think (informal): Who do you think
247 dopy ['dəʊpi] (informal) : stupid
248 prick (slang, taboo): normally: penis, (here): ironical use of the meaning: a miserable person, especially a person in authority
249 'E's ya brother come 'ome (informal): He's your brother, who has come home.
250 incredulously: with disbelief
251 to extend: to reach out
252 slim: thin and small

They shake hands and stare deep into each other's faces, smiling. Brown-black and brown-yellow. They let their happiness soak[253] silently into each other.

Then his cousin Rennie, also tall and slender[254] like a young boomer[255], with bushy red-tinged[256] hair and eager grey eyes, shakes hands. He introduces Billy to his young woman, Phyllis[257], and reminds him who old China Groves and Florrie Waters (his mother's parents) are.

His mother sits silently at the scarred[258] kitchen table. Her wrinkled[259] brown face has been battered around[260], and one of her eyes is sightless. The other stares at his son with a bleak[261] pride of her own.

From that womb[262] I came, Billy thinks, like a flower from the ground or a fledgling[263] from a nest. From out of the reserve[264] I flew.

Where is beauty now?

He remembers his mother as a laughing brown woman, with long black hair in plaits,[265] singing soft songs as she cleaned the house or cooked food. Now she is old and stupid in the mourning[266] of her man.

"So ya came back after all. Ya couldn't come back for ya Dad's funeral[267], but – unna[268]? Ya too good for us mob, I s'pose[269]," she whispers in a thin voice like the mouth organ before he even says hello, then turns her eyes back into her pain.

"It's my birthday, Mum. I wanted to see everybody. No one told me Dad was dead."

Carlton looks up at Billy. I make out ya[270] twenty-one, Billy."

"Yes."

---

253 to soak (fig.): (here): to sink deeply
254 slender: thin in an attractive way
255 boomer (Australian English): large, male kangaroo
256 red-tinged: with just a small amount of red colour
257 Phyllis ['fılıs]
258 scarred: (here): *zerkratzt*
259 wrinkled: with many lines and folds in the skin that are typical of an older person
260 to batter around: to abuse a person with physical violence
261 bleak: offering little hope
262 womb [wu:m]: uterus (*Mutterleib*)
263 fledgling: a young bird that has just learned to fly
264 reserve: area of land set aside by the government for Aborigines and to protect the natural environment
265 plait [plæt]: a long piece of hair, which is divided into three parts and twisted together
266 to mourn [mɔ:n]: to show and feel sadness because s.o. has died
267 funeral: a ceremony for burying a dead person
268 unna (Aboriginal language): "Is that the truth?"
269 s'pose (informal): suppose
270 make out ya (informal): understand you are

"Well, shit, we just gotta 'ave[271] a party." Carlton half-smiles. "We gotta get more drink, but[272]," he adds.

Carlton and Rennie drive off to town in Billy's car. When they leave, Billy feels unsure and alone. His mother just stares at him. Phyllis keeps her eyes glued[273] on the mound[274] of her womb and the grandparents crow[275] to Darcy, camp talk he cannot understand.

The cousins burst through the door with a carton that Carlton drops on the table, then he turns to his brother. His smooth face holds the look of a small child who is about to show his father something he has achieved. His dark lips twitch[276] as they try to keep from smiling.

" 'Appy[277] birthday, Billy, ya ole cunt[278]," Carlton says, and produces a shining gold watch from the ragged[279] pocket of his black jeans.

"It even works, Billy,"' grins Rennie from beside his woman, so Darcy and China laugh.

The laughter swirls[280] around the room like dead leaves from a tree.

They drink. They talk. Darcy goes home and the old people go to bed. His mother has not talked to Billy all night. In the morning he will buy her some pretty curtains for the windows and make a proper door and buy her the best dress in the shop.

They chew on the sweet cud[281] of their past. The memories seep[282] through Billy's skin so he isn't William Woodward the talented football player and artist, but Billy the wild, half-naked boy, with his shock[283] of hair and carefree grin and a covey[284] of girls fluttering around his honey body.

---

271 gotta 'ave (informal): have got to have
272 but: however
273 glued (fig.): (here): fixed, constantly looking at
274 mound (fig.): small hill
275 to crow (fig.): (here): to speak with repeated, high sounds
276 to twitch: to make sudden, quick movements
277 'appy (informal): happy
278 ya ole cunt (slang, taboo): you old cunt: normally *cunt* is a taboo word for vagina or a term used to insult s.o., especially a woman – Here it is used ironically to mean *mate*.
279 ragged ['rægɪd]: old and torn
280 to swirl: to move around quickly in a circle
281 to chew on the cud: normally: *widerkauen* – (here): in the sense of to repeatedly think or talk about s.th.
282 to seep (fig.): to flow slowly through in small amounts
283 shock: thick mass
284 covey ['kʌvi] (fig.): small group of birds, (here): group

Here they are – all three together again, except now young Rennie is almost a father and Carlton has just come from three months' jail. And Billy? He is nowhere.

At last, Carlton yawns[285] and stretches.

"I reckon[286] I'll 'it that bed[287]." Punches[288] his strong brother gently on the shoulder. "See ya t'morrow, Billy, ole kid." He smiles.

Billy camps beside the dying fire. He rolls himself into a bundle of ragged blankets on the floor and stares into the fire. In his mind he can hear his father droning away[289], telling legends that he half-remembered, and his mother softly singing hymns. Voices and memories and woodsmoke drift[290] around him. He sleeps.

He wakes to the sound of magpies carolling[291] in the still trees. Rolls up off the floor and rubs the sleep from his eyes. Gets up and stacks[292] the blankets in a corner, then creeps[293] out to the door.

Carlton's eyes peep[294] out from the blankets on his bed.

"Where ya goin'?" he whispers.

"Just for a walk."

"Catch ya up[295], Billy," he smiles sleepily. With his headband off, his long hair falls every way.

Billy gives a salutation[296] and ducks[297] outside.

A watery sun struggles[298] up over the hills and reflects in the orange puddles[299] that dot[300] the camp. Broken glass winks[301] white, like the bones of dead animals. Several children play with a drum, rolling it at each other and trying to balance on it. Several young men stand around looking at

---

[285] to yawn: *gähnen*
[286] to reckon (informal): (here): to think, to guess
[287] 'it that bed (informal): hit that bed: go to bed
[288] to punch: to hit s.o. with your fist
[289] to drone away: to speak with a low, monotonous tone without stopping
[290] to drift: to be carried away by the currents of wind or water
[291] to carol (fig.): normally: to sing a joyful hymn, (here): to sing in a joyful way
[292] to stack: to neatly place things on top of each other
[293] to creep: to move slowly and quietly
[294] to peep: to look out at s.th. or s.o. from a small opening
[295] catch ya up (informal): I'll catch up with you. – to catch up with s.o.: to reach s.o. who is ahead by going faster
[296] to give a salutation: (here): to gesture with a sign you agree with s.o.'s suggestion
[297] to duck: to lower your body or head to avoid s.th.
[298] to struggle: to try very hard to do s.th. which is difficult
[299] puddle: small amount or water that has collected on the ground after rain
[300] to dot: to be at many different places
[301] to wink: to shine with an unsteady light

Billy's car. He nods[302] at them and they nod back. Billy stumbles over to the ablution block[303]: three bent and rusty showers and a toilet each for men and women. Names and slogans are scribbled[304] on every available space. After washing away the staleness[305] of the beer he heads for the waterhole, where memories of his father linger[306]. He wants – a lot – to remember his father.

He squats[307] there, watching the ripples[308] the light rain makes on the serene[309] green surface. The bird calls from the jumble[310] of green-brown-black bush are sharp and clear, like the echoes of spirits calling to him.

He gets up and wanders back to the humpy. Smoke from fires wisps[311] up into the grey sky.

Just as he slouches[312] to the edge of the clearing, a police van noses its way[313] through the mud and water and rubbish. A pale, hard, supercilious[314] face peers out at him. The van stops.

"Hey, you! Come here!"

The people at the fires watch, from the corner of their eyes, as he idles over[315].

"That your car?"

Billy nods, staring at the heavy, blue-clothed sergeant[316]. The driver growls[317], "What's your name, and where'd you get the car?"

"I just told you it's my car. My name's William Jacob Woodward, if it's any business of yours," Billy flares[318].

---

302 to nod: *nicken*
303 ablution block (formal, humorous): facilities for washing yourself
304 to scribble: to write s.th. quickly and carelessly
305 staleness: state of being tasteless and flat because of being kept open too long
306 to linger: to continue to exist longer than expected
307 to squat: to sit on the ground or floor with your legs bent under your body
308 ripple: small wave on the surface of water
309 serene [sə'ri:n]: quiet and calm
310 jumble: confused mixture
311 to wisp: to move with long, thin lines
312 to slouch [slaʊtʃ]: to move in a lazy way with your shoulders and head bent forward
313 noses its way: moves forward slowly and carefully
314 supercilious [ˌsu:pə'sɪliəs]: showing arrogant pride
315 to idle ['aɪdl] over: to drive slowly to a place
316 sergeant ['sɑ:dʒənt]: policeman between inspector and constable
317 to growl [graʊl]: to say in a low, angry voice
318 to flare (fig.): (here): to suddenly become angry

The sergeant's door opens with an ominous[319] crack[320] as he slowly gets out. He glances[321] down at black Billy, who suddenly feels small and naked.

"You any relation to Carlton?"

"If you want to know –"

"I want to know, you black prick[322]. I want to know everything about you."

"Yeah[323], like where you were last night when the store was broken into, as soon as you come home causing trouble in the pub," the driver snarls[324].

"I wasn't causing trouble, and I wasn't in any robbery. I like the way you come straight down here when there's trouble –"

"If you weren't in the robbery, what's this watch?" the sergeant rumbles[325] triumphantly, and he grabs hold of[326] Billy's hand that has marked so many beautiful marks and painted so many beautiful pictures for the wadgula people. He twists[327] it up behind Billy's back and slams[328] him against the blank[329] blue side of the van. The golden watch dangles[330] between the pink fingers, mocking the stunned[331] man.

"Listen. I was here. You can ask my grandparents or Darcy Goodrich, even," he moans[332]. But inside he knows it is no good.

"Don't give me that[333], Woodward. You bastards stick together like flies on a dunny[334] wall," the driver sneers[335].

---

319 ominous ['ɒmɪnəs]: suggesting that s.th. bad is going to happen soon
320 crack: sudden, loud noise
321 to glance: to look quickly at s.th.
322 prick (slang, taboo): (here): bastard, miserable person
323 yeah (informal): (here): yes
324 to snarl: to speak in an angry and bad-tempered way
325 to rumble: to speak with a deep, resonant sound
326 to grab hold of: to seize
327 to twist: to turn into a position that is not natural or normal
328 to slam: to push with force
329 blank: (here): cold, emotionless
330 to dangle: to hang or swing freely
331 to stun: to shock or surprise so that you cannot think clearly
332 to moan [məʊn]: to make a long, deep sound, expressing unhappiness or suffering (*stöhnen*)
333 Don't give me that ... (informal): Don't tell me nonsense like that.
334 dunny (Australian English, informal): outside toilet
335 to sneer: to smile in a mocking way to show you have no respect for s.o.

Nothing matters any more. Not the trees, flinging[336] their scraggly[337] arms wide in freedom. Not the people around their warm fires. Not the drizzle[338] that drips[339] down the back of his shirt onto his skin. Just this thickset[340], glowering[341] man and the sleek[342] oiled machine[343] with POLICE stencilled[344] on the sides neatly and indestructibly.

"You mongrel[345] black bastard, I'm going to make you – and your fucking[346] brother – jump. You could have killed old Peters last night," the huge man hisses[347] dangerously. Then the driver is beside him, glaring[348] from behind his sunglasses.

"You Woodwards are all the same, thieving boongs[349]. If you think you're such a fighter, beating up old men, you can have a go at[350] the sarge[351] here when we get back to the station."

"Let's get the other one now, Morgan. Mrs Riley said there were two of them."

He is shoved into the back, with a few jabs[352] to hurry him on his way. Hunches[353] miserably in the jolting[354] iron belly[355] as the van revs[356] over to the humpy. Catches a glimpse of[357] his new Kingswood standing in the filth. Darcy, a frightened Rennie and several others lean against it, watching with lifeless eyes. Billy returns their gaze[358] with the look of a

---

336 to fling: to move suddenly and with force
337 scraggly (USA, informal): thin and irregular
338 drizzle: light rain
339 to drip: to fall in small drops
340 thickset: with a strong, heavy body
341 to glower ['glaʊəʳ]: to look in an angry and aggressive way
342 sleek: (here): elegant and shiny
343 machine: i.e. the van
344 to stencil: to make letters or a design on a surface using a thin sheet of metal or thick paper with the letters or design cut out that is painted over
345 mongrel ['mʌŋgrəl] (fig.): a dog that is a mixture of different breeds
346 fucking (slang, taboo): damned
347 to hiss: (here): to say in a quiet, angry way
348 to glare: to look at s.o. in an angry way
349 boong [bu:ŋ:] (Australian English): an insulting term for an Aborigine
350 to have a go at (informal): to start to fight with s.o.
351 sarge (informal): sergeant
352 jab: a sudden, hard hit with a fist (*Faust*)
353 to hunch: to sit with the body drawn or bent together
354 to jolt: to move suddenly and roughly
355 belly (fig.): stomach
356 to rev: to accelerate, to suddenly increase the speed
357 to catch a glimpse of: to look at s.th. or s.o. for a short time
358 gaze: a long. steady look at s.th. or s.o.

cornered[359] dingo[360] who does not understand how he was trapped yet who knows he is about to die. Catches a glimpse of his brother being pulled from the humpy, sad yet sullen[361], eyes downcast[362] staring into the mud of his life – mud that no one can ever escape.

He is thrown into the back of the van.

The van starts up with a satisfied roar[363].

Carlton gives Billy a tired look as though he isn't there, then gives his strange, faint smile.

"Welcome 'ome, brother," he mutters.

1. The following is the lyrics for the song mentioned at the beginning of the short story.
   Who is the "I" in the song? What themes do you find in the song that are similar to the themes in the short story? What is significant about Charlie Pride singing the song?

Detroit City

I want to go home, I want to go home,
Oh Lord, I want to go home,

Last night I went to sleep in Detroit city,
And I dreamed about those cotton fields and home,
I dreamed about my mother,
dear old papa, sister and brother,
And I dreamed about that girl,
whose been waitin' for so long,

I want to go home, I want to go home,
Oh Lord, I want to go home,

Home folks think I'm big in Detroit city,
From the letters that I write they think I'm fine,
But by day I make the cars,
by night I make the bars,

[359] cornered: in a place or situation from which there is no escape
[360] dingo: a wild dog found in Australia
[361] sullen: unwilling to talk because of being bad-tempered
[362] downcast: looking down
[363] roar: (here): loud, deep sound

If only they could read between the lines,
I want to go home, I want to go home,
Oh Lord, I want to go home,

I rode a freight train north to Detroit city,
After all these years I've been wasting my time,
I'll take my foolish pride,
on a southbound freight and ride,
Go on back to the ones,
I've left waitin' so far behind,

I want to go home, I want to go home,
Oh Lord, I want to go home.

Detroit City
Words & Music by Danny Dill & Mel Tillis

2. From what viewpoint is the story told? Why?
3. What tense is used for the narration? Why?
4. Comment on:
   "Act stupid, buddy, an' ya go a lo – ong way in this town."
   Brown-black and brown-yellow.
   And Billy? He is nowhere.
   … staring into the mud of his life – mud that no one can ever escape.
5. How does the author use the natural surroundings?
6. Explain the title of the short story.
7. Comment on the names of the Aborigines.
8. You are a reporter working for the local newspaper. Write an article after seeing Billy at the police station.
9. Compare the racism dealt with in the short story with racism in the USA.

Tim Winton (1960–)

Tim Winton was born in Karrinyup, a suburb of Perth, Western Australia, where he attended primary school. After attending secondary school in Albany he completed his education at the Western Institute of Technology with a degree in creative writing. In his early twenties he already achieved literary fame with his first two novels **An Open Swimmer** (1982) and **Shallows** (1984). Both novels deal with the sea and the relationship of humans to it. In the 1980s he published several collections of stories, of which *Neighbours* appears in **Scission** (1985). Other novels worthy of mention are **That Eye in the Sky** (1986), which reveals a Christian world view, **Cloudstreet** (1991), a post-Second World War family saga, and **Blueback** (1997), a fable much like Antoine de Saint-Exupéry's **The Little Prince**, which returns to the theme of man's relationship to the sea and the destruction of its ecology. He lives in Western Australia with his family.

Neighbours (1985)

When they first moved in, the young couple were wary of[1] the neighbourhood. The street was full of European migrants[2]. It made the newly-weds[3] feel like sojourners[4] in a foreign land. Next door on the left lived a Macedonian[5] family. On the right, a widower[6] from Poland.

The newly-weds' house was small, but its high ceilings and paned[7] windows gave it the feel of an elegant cottage. From his study[8] window, the young man could see out over the rooftops and used-car yards, the Moreton Bay figs[9] in the park where they walked their dog. The neighbours seemed cautious about the dog, a docile[10], moulting[11] collie.

The young man and woman had lived all their lives in the expansive[12] outer suburbs where good neighbours were seldom seen and never heard. The sounds of spitting[13] and washing and daybreak[14] watering[15] came as a shock. The Macedonian family shouted, ranted[16], screamed. It took six months for the newcomers to comprehend[17] the fact that their neighbours were not murdering each other, merely talking. The old Polish man spent most of his day hammering nails into wood only to pull them out again.

---

1 to be wary ['weəri] of: to be careful when dealing with s.o. or s.th. because there may be a danger or problem

2 migrant ['maɪgrənt]: a person who moves from country to another to find work

3 newly-weds: a couple recently married

4 sojourner ['sɒdʒɜ:nə]: a person who stays in a certain place for a short time

5 Macedonian [ˌmæsɪ'dəʊniən]

6 widower: a man whose wife has died

7 paned window: a window that has several separate pieces of glass held together in a frame

8 study: room used for studying, writing, reading, etc.

9 Moreton Bay fig: *Ficus macrophylla*, a large evergreen banyan tree that is a native of most of the eastern coast of Australia. Its common name is derived from Moreton Bay in Queensland, Australia. It is an evergreen tree that can reach heights of 60 m. The trunk can be massive and thick, reaching a diameter of 2.4 m. It is often planted in public parks.

10 docile ['dəʊsaɪl]: quiet and easy to control

11 to moult [məʊlt]: (here): to lose hair

12 expansive: covering a large area

13 to spit: to force liquid or food out of your mouth

14 daybreak: time of day when light first appears

15 watering: i.e. the watering of plants and the lawn

16 to rant: to speak or complain in an angry and loud way

17 to comprehend (formal): to understand

His yard was stacked[18] with salvaged[19] lumber[20]. He added to it, but he did not build with it.

Relations were uncomfortable for many months. The Macedonians raised eyebrows at the late hour at which the newcomers rose in the mornings. The young man sensed their disapproval[21] at his staying home to write his thesis[22] while his wife worked. He watched in disgust[23] as the little boy next door urinated in the street. He once saw him spraying[24] the cat from the back step. The child's head was shaved regularly, he assumed[25], in order to make his hair grow thick. The little boy stood at the fence with only his cobalt eyes showing; it made the young man nervous.

In the autumn, the young couple cleared rubbish from their backyard and turned[26] and manured[27] the soil[28] under the open and measured gaze[29] of the neighbours. They planted leeks[30], onions, cabbage[31], brussel sprouts[32] and broad beans[33] and this caused the neighbours to come to the fence and offer advice about spacing, hilling[34], mulching[35]. The young man resented[36] the interference, but he took careful note of what was said. His wife was bold[37] enough to run a hand over the child's stubble[38] and the big woman with black eyes and butcher's arms gave her a bagful of garlic cloves[39] to plant.

---

[18] to stack: to pile neatly
[19] to salvage: to save damaged parts from a fire, a shipwreck, etc. that can still be used
[20] lumber (AE): large pieces of wood used for building and carpentry
[21] disapproval: *Missbilligung*
[22] thesis ['θiːsəs]: dissertation, scholarly work for an advanced degree
[23] disgust: strong feeling of dislike or disapproval
[24] to spray: *spritzen*
[25] to assume: to suppose
[26] to turn: (here): to cut into the earth and move the loose parts up to the surface
[27] to manure: to spread animal waste onto the soil so that plants grow better
[28] soil [sɔɪl]: top layer of earth in which plants grow
[29] measured gaze: the careful observation
[30] leek: *Lauch*
[31] cabbage: *Kohl*
[32] brussel sprouts: *Rosenkohl*
[33] broad bean: a type of round, pale green bean (*Saubohne*)
[34] to hill: to form a small pile of earth for a plant to grow in
[35] to mulch: to cover the soil or roots of a plant with dead leaves and small pieces of wood as a protection
[36] to resent: to feel bitter or angry about s.th. because you feel it is unfair
[37] bold [bəʊld]: courageous and confident
[38] stubble: short, stiff hair
[39] garlic clove: *Knoblauchzehe*

Not long after, the young man and woman built a henhouse. The neighbours watched it fall down. The Polish widower slid through the fence uninvited and rebuilt it for them. They could not understand a word he said.

As autumn merged into[40] winter and the vermilion[41] sunsets were followed by sudden, dark dusks[42] touched with the smell of woodsmoke and the sound of roosters[43] crowing[44] day's end, the young couple found themselves smiling back at the neighbours. They offered heads of cabbage and took gifts of grappa[45] and firewood. The young man worked steadily at his thesis on the development of the twentieth century novel. He cooked dinners for his wife and listened to her stories of eccentric[46] patients and hospital incompetence. In the street they no longer walked with their eyes lowered. They felt superior[47] and proud when their parents came to visit and to cast shocked glances[48] across the fence.

In the winter they kept ducks, big, silent muscovies[49] that stood about in the rain growing fat. In the spring the Macedonian family showed them how to slaughter and to pluck[50] and to dress[51]. They all sat around on blocks and upturned buckets[52] and told barely[53]-understood stories – the men butchering, the women plucking, as was demanded. In the haze[54] of down[55] and steam and fractured[56] dialogue, the young man and woman felt intoxicated[57]. The cat toyed[58] with severed[59] heads.

---

[40] to merge into: to slowly disappear and reappear in a new form
[41] vermillion [vəˈmɪljən]: bright red
[42] dusk: the time of the day shortly before it is completely dark
[43] rooster (AE): *Hahn*
[44] to crow [krəʊ]: to make a sound like a rooster
[45] grappa: a strong alcoholic drink made from grapes – originally produced in Italy
[46] eccentric: strange, unusual
[47] superior [suːˈpɪəriəʳ]: thinking you are better than others
[48] to cast a glance: to look quickly at s.th. or s.o.
[49] muscovy (duck): a large, dark duck (*Cairina moschata*) originally from Central and South America that is widely kept as a farm animal
[50] to pluck: to pull out the feathers
[51] to dress: to prepare for cooking
[52] bucket: *Eimer*
[53] barely: hardly
[54] haze: air containing s.th. that makes it difficult to see through
[55] down: the soft, fine feathers of a bird
[56] fractured: in bits and pieces
[57] intoxicated: (here): very excited so that you can't think clearly as if having drunk alcohol
[58] to toy: to play
[59] severed: cut off

The child pulled the cat's tail. The newcomers found themselves shouting.

But they had not planned on a pregnancy[60]. It stunned[61] them to be made parents so early. Their friends did not have children until several years after being married – if at all. The young woman arranged for maternity leave[62]. The young man ploughed on[63] with his thesis on the twentieth century novel.

The Polish widower began to build. In the late spring dawns[64], he sank posts[65] and poured[66] cement and began to use his wood. The young couple turned in their bed, cursed[67] him behind his back. The young husband, at times, suspected[68] that the widower was deliberately[69] antagonising[70] them. The young wife threw up[71] in the mornings. Hay fever[72] began to wear him down[73].

Before long the young couple realised that the whole neighbourhood knew of the pregnancy. People smiled tirelessly at them. The man in the deli[74] gave her small presents of chocolates and him packets of cigarettes that he stored at home, not being a smoker. In the summer, Italian women began to offer names. Greek women stopped the young woman in the street, pulled her skirt up and felt her belly[75], telling her it was bound[76] to be a boy. By late summer the woman next door had knitted[77] the baby

---

60 pregnancy: *Schwangerschaft*
61 to stun: to surprise so much that you can't think clearly
62 maternity leave: a period of time when a woman temporarily leaves her job to have a baby
63 to plough [plaʊ] on (fig.): to continue doing s.th. that is difficult
64 dawn: sunrise
65 to sink posts: to push heavy, thick poles into the ground
66 to pour [pɔːʳ]: *gießen*
67 to curse: *fluchen*
68 to suspect: to think that s.o. is planning s.th. bad
69 deliberately: on purpose
70 to antagonise: to do s.th. that gets s.o. angry
71 to throw up: to vomit, to bring the food in the stomach through the mouth
72 hay fever: *Heuschnupfen*
73 to wear s.o. down: to make s.o. weaker, more tired
74 deli (informal): delicatessen, a shop that sells cooked meats and cheeses, and special or unusual foods from other countries
75 belly: stomach
76 bound: likely
77 to knit: *stricken*

a suit, complete with booties[78] and beanie[79]. The young woman felt flattered[80], claustrophobic[81], grateful, peeved[82].

By late summer, the Polish widower next door had almost finished his two-car garage. The young man could not believe that a man without a car would do such a thing, and one evening as he was considering making a complaint[83] about the noise, the Polish man came over with barrowfuls[84] of woodscraps[85] for their fire.

Labour[86] came abruptly. The young man abandoned[87] the twentieth century novel for the telephone. His wife began to black[88] the stove[89]. The midwife[90] came and helped her finish the job while he ran about making statements that sounded like queries[91]. His wife hoisted[92] her belly about the house, supervising[93] his movements. Going outside for more wood, he saw, in the last light of the day, the faces at each fence. He counted twelve faces. The Macedonian family waved and called out what sounded like their best wishes.

As the night deepened, the young woman dozed[94] between contractions[95], sometimes walking, sometimes shouting. She had a hot bath and began to eat ice and demand liverwurst. Her belly rose, uterus[96] flexing[97] downward. Her sweat[98] sparkled[99], the gossamer[100] highlit[101] by movement

---

78 booty: a knitted sock for babies
79 beanie (USA): a round, small, close-fitting hat
80 to flatter: to say s.th. nice to a person because you want to please this person or want s.th. from him or her
81 claustrophobic [ˌklɔːstrəˈfəʊbɪk]: afraid of being in a small, confined place
82 peeved: annoyed
83 complaint: a statement that you are not satisfied about s.th. (*Beschwerde*)
84 barrowful: what a wheelbarrow (*Schubkarre*) can hold
85 woodscraps: small pieces of woods that are left over
86 labour: (here): *die Wehen*
87 to abandon: to leave s.th. you are responsible for with no intention of returning
88 to black: to polish with blacking (a kind of paste)
89 stove: wood or coal stove made of iron
90 midwife: a woman, who is trained to help women give birth to babies
91 query: question
92 to hoist: to raise into a higher position
93 to supervise: to be in charge of s.o. and make sure that everything is done correctly
94 to doze: to sleep lightly for a short time
95 contractions: *Geburtswehen*
96 uterus [ˈjuːtərəs]: *Gebärmutter*
97 to flex: to contract
98 sweat [swet]: *Schweiß*
99 to sparkle: to shine brightly with small flashes of light
100 gossamer (fig.): (here): the layer of sweat that looked like the thin threads of a spider web
101 to highlight, highlit, highlit: to emphasise, to make easier to notice

and firelight. The night grew older. The midwife crooned[102]. The young man rubbed his wife's back, fed her ice and rubbed her lips with oil.

And then came the pushing. He caressed[103] and stared and tried not to shout. The floor trembled[104] as the young woman bore down[105] in a squat[106]. He felt the power of her, the sophistication[107] of her. She strained[108]. Her face mottled[109]. She kept at it, push after push, assaulting[110] some unseen barrier, until suddenly it was smashed[111] and she was through. It took his wind away to see the look on the baby's face as it was suddenly passed up to the breast. It had one eye on him. It found the nipple[112]. It trailed[113] cord[114] and vernix smears[115] and its mother's own sweat. She gasped[116] and covered the tiny buttocks[117] with a hand. A boy, she said. For a second, the child lost the nipple and began to cry. The young man heard shouting outside. He went to the back door. On the Macedonian side of the fence, a small queue of bleary[118] faces looked up, cheering, and the young man began to weep[119]. The twentieth century novel had not prepared him for this.

1. Why are the names of the characters not mentioned?

2. What is the viewpoint of the story? What tense is used in the narration?

---

102 to croon: to sing quietly and gently
103 to caress: to touch gently, showing affection
104 to tremble: to shake
105 to bear, bore, borne down: to quickly move down
106 squat: a sitting position with the legs bent up under the body
107 sophistication: having a lot of experience of the world
108 to strain: to make a great effort to do s.th. with all your strength
109 mottled: with marks of different colours and shapes
110 to assault: to attack violently
111 to smash: to break through
112 nipple: *Brustwarze*
113 to trail: to pull or leave s.th. behind s.o. or s.th.
114 cord: *Nabelschnur*
115 vernix smears: i.e. traces of *Vernix caseosa*, also known as vernix, a waxy or cheese-like white substance found on the skin of human babies immediately after birth
116 to gasp: to take a quick, deep breath with your mouth open
117 buttocks: the part of the body you sit on
118 bleary: (here): not able to see clearly because of tears
119 to weep: to cry, normally when unhappy or in grief

3. Comment on the sentence structure.

4. Explain:

   The young man worked steadily at his thesis on the development of the twentieth century novel.

   The twentieth century novel had not prepared him for this.

   They felt superior and proud when their parents came to visit and to cast shocked glances across the fence.

   ... the men butchering, the women plucking, as was demanded.

   It stunned them to be made parents so early. Their friends did not have children until several years after being married – if at all.

   His wife began to black the stove.

   He felt the power of her, the sophistication of her.

   ... and the young man began to weep.

5. Contrast and compare the women in the short story. Consider the women in the other short stories.

6. Explain "the other" and "othering" in the context of this short story. Hint: think of a reversal of roles. Compare the clash of cultures in this short story with *My Son the Fanatic* by Hanif Kureishi in **The Many Voices of English**, Diesterweg, 2005.

7. Can you determine a Christian world view in this short story? (Think of the nativity scene in the New Testament.)

8. Examine the details of the birth. What conclusions can you draw?

9. Comment on the following statement with specific references to the short story:

   The story is told with a cool detachment[120] leavened[121]
   with occasional flashes of dry humour[122].

---

120 detachment: *Distanz*, *Abstand*

121 to leaven ['levən] (fig:): to make s.th. more interesting by adding s.th.

122 p. 19 in *Introduction* in **The Penguin Best Australian Short Stories**, Mary Lord, editor, Penguin Books Australia, Ringwood, Victoria, Australia, 1991

Information about Australia[1]

OFFICIAL NAME:
Commonwealth of Australia

Geography:
area: 7.7 million sq. km. (3 million sq. mi.) — **Germany:** 357,021 sq. km. (137,847 sq. mi.)

Cities (2008)**:** capital – Canberra (pop. 345,000). Other cities – Sydney (4.4 million), Melbourne (3.9 million), Brisbane (1.95 million), Perth (1.6 million), Adelaide (1.2 million), Darwin (120,000), Hobart (209,000)

Terrain: varied, but generally low-lying

Climate: relatively dry and subject to drought[2], ranging from temperate in the south to tropical in the far north – Southeastern Australia has a climate similar to northwestern Europe.

People:
Population (2009 estimated)**:** 21.8 million — **Germany:** 82 million (2008)

Annual population growth rate: 1.7% — **Germany:** – 0.1% (2005–2010 per annum[3])

Ethnic groups: European 92%, Asian 6%, Aboriginal 2%. **Germany:** primarily German; 2.6 million citizens and residents of Turkish descent; Danish minority in the north, Sorbian (Slavic) minority in the east; 7.257 million foreign residents (2007); 18% of Germany's inhabitants have an immigrant background (2008).

Religions (2006): Catholic 26%, Anglican 19%, other Christian 19%, other non-Christian 1%, Buddhist 2.1%, Islam 1.7%, no religion 19%, and not stated 12%

Germany: Protestants (26 million); Roman Catholics (26 million); approximately 3.5 million Muslims

---

[1] Australia: from the Latin (*Terra*) *Australis*: Southern (Land)
[2] drought [draʊt]: a long period of time without rain
[3] per annum (Latin): per year

120° East of Greenwich
125°
130°
135°
140°
10°
15°
20°
25°
30°
35°
40°
115°
120°
125°
130°
135°
140°
Indian Ocean
Darwin
Katherine
Mount Hann 776 m
Kununurra
Kimberley Plateau
Derby
Broome
Fitzroy
NORTHERN TERRITORY
Port Hedland
Great Sandy Desert
Fortescue
Mount Bruce 1226 m
Ashburton
Gascoyne
Tropic of Capricorn
Carnarvon
Mount Fraser 802 m
Gibson Desert
Mount Zeil 1510 m
Macdonnell Ranges
Alice Springs
Mount Olga 1069 m
Ayers Rock 867 m
Mount Woodroffe 1440 m
Great Victoria Desert
Coober Pedy
WESTERN AUSTRALIA
SOUTH AUS
Geraldton
Kalgoorlie
Nullarbor Plain
Eucla Motels
Perth
Fremantle
Bluff Knoll 1109 m
Albany
Indian Ocean
Population of cities and towns
under 50,000
50,000-500,000
over 500,000
Heights in m
> 2000
1000 - 2000
500 - 1000
200 - 500
0 - 200
< 0
Desert
Time zone
Time in Germany
0 mile 250 500
0 km 500 1000

Coral Sea
Great Barrier Reef
Pacific Ocean
Tropic of Capricorn
Tasman Sea
QUEENSLAND
NEW SOUTH WALES
VICTORIA
TASMANIA
AUSTRALIAN CAPITAL TERRITORY
Great Dividing Range
Cairns
Mount Bartle Frere 1622 m
Townsville
Mount Isa
Mount Dalrymple 1277 m
Mackay
Rockhampton
Gladstone
Mount Ackland 975 m
Bundaberg
Ipswich
Brisbane
Toowoomba
Gold Coast
Lismore
Round Mtn. 1586 m
Tamworth
Taree
Dubbo
Maitland
Newcastle
Orange
Bathurst
Sydney
Wollongong
Cootamundra
Wagga Wagga
Albury
Canberra
Mount Kosciusko 2228 m
Bendigo
Ballarat
Melbourne
Geelong
Hobart
Adelaide
Whyalla
St. Mary Peak 1188 m
Broken Hill
Lake Eyre
Cooper Creek
Flinders
Georgina
Thomson
Warrego
Balonne
Namoi
Darling
Lachlan
Murray
Murrumbidgee
TRALIA
mpson
sert
Hamburg
Hannover
Berlin
Köln
Dresden
Frankfurt
Stuttgart
München
145°
150°
155°
160°
165°
170°
10°
15°
20°
25°
30°
35°
40°

Languages: primarily English

Education:
literacy: over 99% **Germany:** 99%

Health: infant mortality rate: 4.7/1,000; life expectancy: males 78 yrs., females 83 yrs.
Germany: infant mortality rate (2008 estimated): 4.03/1,000; life expectancy (2008 est.): males 76.11 years, females 82.26 years

Work force (10.8 million)**:** agriculture: 3.3%; mining: 1.5%; manufacturing: 9.8%; retail trade[4]: 11.3%; public administration, defense, and safety: 6%; construction: 9.2%

Government:
Type: constitutional monarchy: democratic, federal-state system
Constitution: passed by the British Parliament on July 9, 1900
Independence (federation): January 1, 1901
Branches: Executive: Queen Elizabeth II (head of state, represented by a governor general); the monarch appoints the governor general on the advice of the prime minister. Legislative: bicameral[5] Parliament (76-member Senate, 150-member House of Representatives) The governor general appoints the prime minister (generally the leader of the party which holds the majority in the House of Representatives) and appoints ministers on the advice of the prime minister. Judicial: independent judiciary
Administrative subdivisions: six states and two territories
Political parties: Australian Labor, Liberal, the Greens, the Nationals, and Family First. The Australian Labor Party currently forms the government.
Suffrage[6]: universal and compulsory 18 and over

Economy:
GDP[7] (2009–2010 estimated): A$1.17 trillion (US $893.6 billion).
Germany: GDP (2007): US $3.317 trillion

---

[4] retail trade: *Einzelhandel*
[5] bicameral: with two houses
[6] suffrage: the right to vote
[7] GDP: Gross Domestic Product (*Bruttoinlandsprodukt*)

Trade:
exports (US $178.9 billion, 2008 estimate): coal, iron ore, gold, meat, wool, alumina, wheat, machinery and transport equipment
Major markets: Japan, China, South Korea, U.S. (US $10.7 billion), and New Zealand
Imports (US $187.2 billion, 2008 estimate): machinery and transport equipment, computers and office machines, telecommunication equipment and parts; crude oil[8] and petroleum products
Major suppliers: China, United States (US $23.96 billion), Japan, Singapore, and Germany

People:

Australia's indigenous[9] inhabitants, a hunting-gathering people collectively referred to today as Aboriginals and Torres Straits Islanders, arrived more than 40,000 years ago. Although their technical culture remained static – depending on wood, bone, stone tools and weapons – their spiritual and social life was highly complex. Most spoke several languages, and confederacies sometimes linked widely scattered[10] tribal groups. Indigenous population density[11] ranged from one person per square mile along the coasts to one person per 35 square miles in the arid interior (also known as The Outback). When Captain James Cook claimed Australia for Great Britain in 1770, the native population may have numbered 300,000 in as many as 500 tribes speaking many different languages. In 2006 the indigenous population was approximately 517,200, representing about 2.5% of the population. Since the end of World War II, the government and the public have made efforts to be more responsive to Aboriginal rights and needs, most recently with former Prime Minister Kevin Rudd's historic apology to the indigenous people in February 2008. His apology focused on the lost generation of Aborigine children, many of mixed race, who were forcibly removed from their families and placed in religious institutions. Indeed, in the past, the disappearance of Aborigines as a distinct race was considered a desirable goal by many politicians.

---

8 crude oil: *Rohöl*
9 indigenous [ɪnˈdɪdʒɪnəs]: native
10 widely scattered: very far apart from each other
11 density: *Dichte*

At first – at the end of the 18th century and the beginning of the next – the native population (called Aborigines by the end of the 19th century) was purposely reduced in size by wholesale[12] slaughter or succumbed to[13] diseases imported from Europe. They were later forced into a programme of assimilation. Alcoholism, drug abuse, and child neglect were the result. Parallels to the European settlement of the New World can be found.

To quote *The New York Times*:

> Until the 1960s, Australian governments tried to absorb Aborigines into the larger, European-based culture. In the most tragic policy of assimilation, state and church officials removed tens of thousands of Aboriginal children, often forcibly, from their families and placed them with white families or in institutions.
> But legal equality in 1967 – along, eventually, with almost complete autonomy across territories ceded to[14] Aboriginal communities – did not translate into a better life for most Aborigines. As equal rights gave Aboriginal communities access[15] to alcohol and semi-monthly welfare payments, health and education standards have continued to decline over the decades. Life expectancy remains 17 years shorter than for other Australians.
> In 2007, the conservative government of Prime Minister John Howard took back a lot of that autonomy in the Northern Territory [...] by seizing direct control over alcohol and welfare. That policy has been maintained by the liberal government of Prime Minister Kevin Rudd [...]
> Western Australia recently started controlling welfare payments in some areas [...] Welfare recipients suspected of child neglect[16] can have 70 percent of their benefits[17] restricted to paying for essentials like food, rent and utilities[18], a strategy intended to reduce their purchase of alcohol.[19]

---

12 wholesale: large scale

13 to succumb [sə'kʌm] to: (here): to not be able to prevent an infection because of a lack of immunity

14 to cede to (formal): to give s.o. the control of s.th.

15 access ['ækses]: *Zugang*

16 neglect: the fact of not giving enough care

17 benefits (plural): money paid by the state to people in need

18 utilities (plural): gas, electricity, water

19 *Facing a Crisis, Aborigines Stage Interventions of Their Own* by Norimitisu Onishi, *New York Times*, July 5, 2009, http://www.nytimes.com/2009/07/05/world/asia/05australia.html?_r=1&hp

Immigration has been vital to Australia's development since the beginning of European settlement in 1788. For generations, most settlers came from the British Isles, and the people of Australia are still predominantly of British or Irish origin.

Because of the prevalence[20] of racist sentiment on the part of the northern European majority non-white immigrants were essentially excluded by the restrictions of the 1901 Immigration Restriction Act. Non-white immigrants were often seen as a threat to working conditions in Australia and to Australia's British character.

These policies remained in place until after World War Two, when the government implemented[21] migration schemes that actively sought first British, then European, migrants. Since then, the face of Australia has changed remarkably. While large numbers of migrants have continued to come from traditional sources like the United Kingdom and New Zealand, there have been large numbers of people from countries as diverse as Italy, Greece, China, Vietnam, India, and Lebanon. Since the end of World War II, Australia's population has more than doubled.

Australia's humanitarian and refugee program of about 13,000 per year is in addition to other immigration programmes. In recent years, refugees from Africa, the Middle East, and Southwest Asia have comprised the largest element in Australia's refugee program. Although Australia has scarcely more than three people per square kilometer, it is one of the world's most urbanised countries, especially along the southeastern coast with its temperate climate. Less than 2.5% of the population lives in remote or very remote areas.

The first decade of the 21st century has witnessed the repeated flare-up[22] of racially motivated violence in such urban centres as Melbourne and Sydney, directed mostly against immigrants from the Near East and South Asia. Notable race riots took place in 2009 and in 2005 when gangs of young white men began attacking people of Middle Eastern appearance in Sydney's beach suburb Cronulla[23]. One should be careful, however, not to generalise that all Australians are racist or xenophobic[24].

---

20 prevalence: s.th. that is very common at a particular time

21 to implement: to carry out

22 flare-up: sudden burst

23 Cf. http://www.guardian.co.uk/world/2005/dec/12/australia

24 xenophobic [ˌzenəˈfəʊbɪk]: disliking or fearing people from a foreign country

Cultural Achievements

Much of Australia's culture is derived from European roots, but distinctive Australian features have evolved from the environment, Aboriginal culture, and the influence of Australia's neighbors. The vigor[25] and originality of the arts in Australia – film, opera, music, painting, theater, dance, and crafts[26] – have achieved international recognition.

History

Australia was uninhabited until stone-culture peoples arrived, perhaps by boat across the waters separating the island from the Indonesia archipelago more than 40,000 years ago. Portuguese, Spanish, Dutch, and English explorers observed the island before 1770, when Captain Cook explored the east coast and claimed it for Great Britain.

On January 26, 1788 (now celebrated as Australia Day), the First Fleet under Captain Arthur Phillip landed at Sydney, and formal proclamation of the establishment of the Colony of New South Wales followed on February 7. Many, but by no means all, of the first settlers were convicts, some condemned for offenses that today would often be thought trivial. From the mid-19th century on convict transportation to Australia significantly declined; the last ship to arrive was in 1868. The discovery of gold in 1851, in many ways similar to the California Gold Rush of 1848/49, led to increased population and trade. Many linguists believe that Australian English was profoundly influenced by the American English spoken by the many gold seekers who arrived from America.

The six colonies that now constitute the states of the Australian Commonwealth were established in the following order: New South Wales, 1788; Tasmania, 1825; Western Australia, 1829; South Australia, 1836; Victoria, 1851; and Queensland, 1859. Settlement preceded these dates in most cases.

During the second half of the 19th century an increasing sense of an Australian identity and increasing anti-British sentiment (notably, among Irish immigrants) led to the desire to establish Australia as an independent nation under a Federation. Not wishing to repeat the mis-

---

[25] vigor ['vɪgə]: vitality

[26] crafts: handiwork

takes that had led to the loss of the American colonies, and with the experience of having already granted self-government to Canada, the British Government sensibly entered into discussions with Australian representatives. These amicable discussions resulted in the British Government's adoption of an act to constitute the Commonwealth of Australia in 1900, effective January 1, 1901. In 1911, control of the Northern Territory was transferred from South Australia to the Commonwealth. Also that year, the Australian Capital Territory (where the national capital, Canberra, is located), was established. The Northern Territory and Australian Capital Territory were granted self-government in 1978 and 1988, respectively.

The Battle of Gallipoli (Turkey) in 1915 during World War One proved to be a turning point in Australian and New Zealand self-perception. Though the battle resulted in a retreat[27], Australian and New Zealand soldiers were considered heroes – highlighted by the qualities Australians and New Zealanders so cherished[28]: courage, ingenuity[29], good humour, mateship[30], and a disdain[31] for the British class system.

Since April 25, 1916 Anzac Day (ANZAC being an acronym[32] for the **Australian and New Zealand Army Corps**) has been annually celebrated in Australia and New Zealand in memory of all Australian and New Zealand soldiers killed in action. Recently, there has been some criticism of Anzac Day because of its purported[33] overemphasis on white soldiers. The 1981 Australian film, *Gallipoli*, portrays Australian participation in The Battle of Gallipoli with a striking feel for period detail.

The first federal Parliament was opened at Melbourne in May 1901 by the Duke of York (later King George V). In May 1927, the seat of government was transferred to Canberra. The first session of Parliament in Canberra was opened by another Duke of York (later King George VI). Australia passed the Statute of Westminster Adoption Act on October 9, 1942 (in effect as of September 3, 1939), which officially established Australia's

---

[27] retreat: withdrawal because of defeat

[28] to cherish: to love very much and want to protect

[29] ingenuity [ˌɪndʒɪˈnjuːəti]: inventiveness

[30] mateship (Australian): friendship, especially between men

[31] disdain: contempt, strong dislike

[32] acronym [ˈækrənɪm]: word formed from the first letters of words that make up a name

[33] purported: supposed

complete autonomy in both internal and external affairs and formalised a situation that had existed for years. The Australia Act (effective March 3, 1986) eliminated almost all remaining vestiges[34] of British legal authority. Still, most Australians are willing to accept the British Monarch as the titular[35] head of their government and have retained the British flag in the corner of their own national flag.

Government

The Commonwealth government was created with a Constitution patterned partly on the U.S. Constitution, although it does not include a "bill of rights." Powers of the Commonwealth are specifically defined in the Constitution, and the residual[36] powers remain with the states. Proposed changes to the Constitution must be approved by the Parliament and the people, via[37] a referendum.

Australia is an independent nation within the Commonwealth. Queen Elizabeth II is the head of state and since 1973 has been officially named "Queen of Australia." The Queen is represented federally by a governor general and in each state by a governor. By convention, the governor general generally acts on the advice of the prime minister and other ministers. However the governor general has "reserve powers," including the power to dismiss ministers, last exercised[38] in 1975.

The federal Parliament is bicameral, consisting of a 76-member Senate and a 150-member House of Representatives. Twelve senators from each state are elected for 6-year terms, with half elected every 3 years. Each territory has two senators who are elected for 3-year terms, concurrent with[39] that of the House. Seats in the House of Representatives are allocated[40] among the states and territories roughly in proportion to population. The two chambers have equal powers, except all proposals for raising taxes or expenditures must be introduced in the House of Representatives. The leader of the political party or coalition of parties that wins a majority of

---

[34] vestige: trace
[35] titular: having a particular title or status with no real power
[36] residual: remaining
[37] via: by means of
[38] to exercise: to make use of
[39] concurrent with: happening at the same time
[40] to allocate: to give officially for a certain purpose

the seats in the House of Representatives is named prime minister. Political power is in the hands of the prime minister and the cabinet, who are also responsible to the Parliament, of which they must be elected members. General elections are held at least once every three years.

Heading the court system is the High Court of Australia. Much like the Supreme Court in the USA, it is the last court of appeals and can decide if cases before it conform to the Australian constitution.

Political Conditions

The four major parties are: the Liberal Party (LP), representing urban business and mining interests, and its smaller coalition partner, the Nationals, representing rural interests, the Australian Labor Party (ALP), representing workers, trade unions, and left-of-center groups, and the Greens Party, being more concerned with environmental questions. While the ALP, founded by labor unions, traditionally had been moderately socialist in its policies and approaches[41] to social issues, today it is best described as a social democratic party. All political groups are tied by tradition to welfare programmes.

Economy:

Australia's economy is dominated by its services sector, yet it is the agricultural and mining sectors that account for the bulk[42] of Australia's exports. Australia's comparative advantage in the export of primary products is a reflection of the natural wealth of the Australian continent and its small domestic market; 21 million people occupy a continent the size of the United States, not including Alaska and Hawaii. The relative size of the manufacturing sector has been declining for several decades, but has now steadied at around 10% of GDP. Australia currently exports more than it imports because of the increasing demand on the part of China for its ore and coal (with an increase in their price), while at the same time there has been a drop in prices for imports for manufactured goods, mainly from China.

---

41 approach: way of dealing with s.th.

42 bulk [bʌlk]: main part

Being a leading coal and iron ore exporter and a major supplier to Asian economies, especially to China, has been perceived to have a downside. Australia's environmental movement has long been uncomfortable with the country's prominent role in supplying the mineral and energy needs of other countries. Of great concern is the fact that Australia produces more per capita[43] CO_2 pollution than any other country in the world. Efforts to reduce CO_2 emission have been hampered[44] by the domestic coal industry.

After a number of environmental catastrophes caused by freighters beaching on the Great Barrier Reef, environmentalists and the Greens Party are insisting on much more stringent[45] laws to prevent any such future incidents. There is also increasing concern about the exploitation of Australia's natural resources by foreign powers.

For more information and updates go to: http://www.state.gov/r/pa/ei/bgn/2698.htm

– based on information from the U.S. Department of State that is in the public domain

---

[43] per capita (Latin): *pro Kopf*
[44] to hamper: to hinder
[45] stringent: strict

The Historical Roots of Transportation

[...] Transportation – forced exile, in plain English – had undeniable merits[1]. It preserved[2] the Royal Prerogative[3] of Mercy[4], as the felon[5] was left alive. At the same time he was removed from the realm[6] as completely, if not as permanently, as any hanged man. Transportation got rid of the prison as well as the prisoners. It supplied Britain with a large labor force, consisting entirely of people who, having forfeited[7] their rights, could be sent to distant colonies of a growing Empire to work at jobs that no free settler would do. Free-born Englishmen had always disliked the idea of laboring bands of convicts[8] engaged on[9] public works at home. A bill of 1752 introducing public chain-gang labor as punishment for criminals was rejected[10] by the Lords[11] partly because security was too great a problem, but mainly because the sight of chain gangs in public places was felt to be degrading[12]. How could onlookers distinguish[13] such a punishment from outright[14] slavery? In the New World, there would be no such problem.

The germ[15] of the transportation system lay in a law of 1597, 39[16] Eliz[17]. c.[18] 4[19], "An Acte[20] for Punyshment[21] of Rogues[22], Vagabonds[23]

1 merit: positive characteristic
2 to preserve: to keep intact
3 prerogative: special right
4 mercy: *Gnade*
5 felon [ˈfelən]: a person who has committed a serious crime
6 realm [relm] (old-fashioned): kingdom
7 to forfeit [ˈfɔːfɪt]: to lose
8 convict: person found guilty of a crime and sent to prison
9 engaged on: employed for
10 to reject: to refuse to accept
11 Lords: the House of Lords
12 degrading: (here): unacceptable because of being too inhumane
13 to distinguish: to determine the difference
14 outright: complete, total
15 germ: the early stage of s.th. that later develops
16 39: i.e. the 39th year of the reign of Queen Elizabeth I
17 Eliz.: referring to Queen Elizabeth I
18 c.: chapter: (here): act or law
19 4: i.e. the fourth act passed in that year
20 Acte (old English spelling): act or law
21 punyshment (old English spelling): punishment
22 rogue [rəʊg] (old-fashioned): dishonest or worthless person
23 vagabond: person without a home or job who begs for food or money

and Sturdy[24] Beggars." In essence[25], it declared that obdurate[26] idlers[27] "shall ... be banished out of this Realm ... and shall be conveyed[28] to such parts beyond the seas as shall be ... assigned[29] by the Privy Council[30]." If a "Rogue so banished" returned to England without permission, he would be hanged.

It was through this act that in the seventeenth century, convicts under commuted[31] death sentences were sent across the Atlantic to labor on the plantations of the Virginia Company. Sir Thomas Dale, Marshal of Virginia, took three hundred "disorderly persons" with him in 1611, but they turned out so "profane[32] and mutinous[33], ... diseased and crazed that not sixty of them may be employed." Still, bad labor was better than none in the New World; the Indians could not be enslaved, while the English gentlemen of the Virginia Company had an extreme distaste for manual work. Soon Dale was asking for two thousand more convicts. "All offenders[34] out of the common gaols[35] condemned to die should be sent for three years to the Colony; so do the Spaniards people the Indies." And from 1618 onward, a steady infusion[36] of felons came to England's embryo settlements in the New World, to Puritan Massachusetts as well as to the tidewater[37] settlements of the South. Most of them were common criminals. Some were Scots and English prisoners-of-war taken by Cromwell[38] at the battles of Dunbar (1650) and Worcester (1651); others – mostly shipped to the sugar plantations of Jamaica and Barbados in the

---

[24] sturdy: healthy, strong
[25] in essence: essentially
[26] obdurate (formal): unchangeable
[27] idler: person who refuses to work
[28] to convey (formal): to send
[29] to assign: to determine
[30] Privy Council: council appointed by a monarch to advise him/her
[31] commuted: replaced by another punishment other than death
[32] profane: lacking any respect for religion
[33] mutinous: refusing to obey orders
[34] offender: person who has committed a crime
[35] gaol (BE): jail
[36] infusion (fig., ironic): the act of adding s.th. to s.th. else in order to make it stronger or more successful
[37] tidewater: area of land near the coast
[38] Cromwell: Oliver Cromwell (1599–1658), English general and statesman. A Puritan and very anti-Roman Catholic, he was an effective leader of the parliamentary army in the Civil War. After the execution of King Charles I he defeated Royalists in Scotland and Ireland, and became Lord Protector of the Commonwealth (1653–1658).

1650s – were Irishmen who had been so unwise as to resist the invasion of the Lord Protector[39].

After 1717, transportation was stepped up and rendered[40] fully official by a new act, 4 Geo. I.[41] c. 11, which provided[42] that minor offenders[43] could be transported for seven years to America instead of being flogged[44] and branded[45], while men on commuted capital[46] sentences (recipients of the King's Mercy) might be sent for fourteen. English jailers did excellent business by selling these luckless colonists to shipping contractors[47], who in turn sold them (or, to be legally precise, the rights to their labor during their seven or fourteen years) to plantation-owners in the Caribbean and America. For the next sixty years, about 40,000 people suffered this thinly disguised[48] form of slavery: 30,000 men and women from Great Britain, 10,000 from Ireland. This steady drainage[49] of felons, averaging fewer than 700 people a year, kept the crowded jails of England from crisis.

But after 1775, the crisis could no longer be postponed[50]. The American colonies rebelled. One result of the revolution was that the British could no longer send its convicts there. The American air filled with nobly turned[51] resolutions[52] against accepting criminals from England, for a new republic must not be polluted with the Crown's offal[53]. This was cant[54], since the American economy was already heavily dependent on slavery. The real point was that the trade in black slaves had turned white convict

---

39 invasion of the Lord Protector: Cromwell's invasion of Ireland that resulted in the slaughter of many Roman Catholics
40 to render (formal): to make
41 Geo.: referring to King George I of Great Britain
42 to provide: to state
43 minor offender: a person who has not committed a serious crime
44 to flog: to whip
45 to brand: to place a permanent mark on the skin with a hot iron
46 capital: death
47 contractor: a person or company that has a contract to do work or provide goods or services for another company
48 thinly disguised [dɪsˈgaɪzd]: not very well hidden, easily discovered
49 drainage (fig., ironic): the process of making s.th. empty or dry by removing all the liquid from it
50 to postpone: to delay, to do at a later time
51 nobly turned: with expressions of high moral ideals
52 resolution:] a formal statement of an opinion agreed on by a council or committee
53 offal [ˈɒfəl]: refuse, rubbish
54 cant: insincere talk, hypocrisy

labor into an economic irrelevance. On the eve[55] of the American Revolution, 47,000 African slaves were arriving in America every year – more than English jails had sent across the Atlantic in the preceding half-century. Beside this labor force, the work of white indentured[56] convicts was inconsequential[57]; the Republic did not need it.

As soon as the American outlet was stopped up, English prisons began to overflow. At first, the Crown did nothing about this. The Americans would surrender sooner or later, and then the convict transports could ply[58] the Atlantic again. In July 1783, only a month before Britain was forced to recognize the United States at Versailles, George III wrote to Lord North[59]: "Undoubtedly the Americans cannot expect nor ever will receive any favour from Me, but the permitting them to obtain Men unworthy to remain in this Island I shall certainly consent to[60]."

So the English did not enlarge their prisons and in 1776 they found a compromise. The idea of forced convict labor on public works no longer seemed so tainted[61] with slavery. It was dusted off[62] and Lord North drew it up as 16 Geo. III[63], c. 43, known as the Hulks[64] Act, a stopgap[65] meant to last only until the American insurgents[66] were crushed[67].

The Thames and the southern naval ports of England were dotted[68] with hulks – old troop transports and men-o'-war[69], their masts and rigging[70] gone, rotting[71] at anchor, but still afloat and theoretically habitable. Con-

---

[55] eve: the period immediately before an event
[56] indentured: forced to work for an employer for a certain period of time
[57] inconsequential: not worth considering, unimportant
[58] to ply: to travel regularly along a route
[59] Lord North (1732–1792): British Prime Minister (1770–1782)
[60] to consent to: to agree to
[61] to taint (formal): to damage or spoil the quality of s.th. or the opinion that people have of s.o. or s.th.
[62] to dust off (fig.): to use s.th. again that has been left unnoticed and unused for a long time
[63] Geo. III: referring to King George III of Great Britain
[64] hulk: the main part of a ship that is no longer used for sailing
[65] stopgap: s.th. you do until you find s.th. better
[66] insurgent: rebel
[67] to crush (fig.): to defeat
[68] to dot: to spread over a wide area
[69] man-o'-war: warship
[70] rigging: ropes used for the sails and to support the masts
[71] to rot: *verotten*

victs sentenced[72] to be transported would now be kept on them until the government decided where to send them; this would relieve[73] the bursting land prisons. Tactfully, the Hulks Act did not mention the revolt of the American colonists. It made a virtue of necessity[74] by noting that transportation had deprived[75] England of people "whose labour might be useful to the Community." These men would now be set "to Hard Labour ... cleansing the River *Thames.*" Thus the felons "might be reclaimed[76]."

But the convicts jammed[77] on the hulks were no more reclaimed than the Thames was cleansed. By 1790 their number was rising by about one thousand a year. Not only had the problem of security become acute[78], but typhus was by then endemic[79] and the prospect of general infection terrified free citizens outside. The authorities would have done almost anything to get rid of the criminals their laws had created. Clearly, transportation must begin again – but to where? They chose the least imaginable spot on earth, which had been visited only once by white men. It was Australia, their new, vast, lonely possession, a useless continent at the rim[80] of the world, whose eastern coast had been mapped by Captain Cook in 1770. From there, the convicts would never return. The names of Newgate and Tyburn[81], arch-symbols[82] of the vengeance[83] of property, were now joined by a third: Botany Bay[84].

Robert Hughes, **The Fatal Shore**, Vintage, Random House, London, 2003, pp. 40 – 42, reprinted on the basis of Paragraph 46 of the German copyright laws

---

72 to sentence: to declare in court what the punishment for a guilty person will be
73 to relieve: to make a problem less serious
74 to make a virtue of necessity: to make s.th. necessary but unpleasant seem like the right thing to do
75 to deprive: to prevent s.o. from having s.th. important
76 to reclaim: (here): to make a criminal a useful citizen again
77 to jam: to pack into a small space
78 acute: very serious
79 endemic: present within a certain area
80 rim: edge
81 Newgate, Tyburn: Newgate, main prison in London until 1902; Tyburn, place in London of execution by hanging until 1783
82 arch-symbol: excellent, best symbol
83 vengeance ['vendʒəns]: *Rache*
84 Botany Bay: Botany Bay was the site of Captain Cook's first landing on the continent of Australia between 1770 and 1771. After 1788 and well into the 19th century it was used as a settlement for convicts.

1. What similarities do you find in this excerpt, written approximately 100 years later, with *How Muster-Master Stoneman Earned His Breakfast*?

2. What is meant by "arch-symbols of the vengeance of property?"

3. What do you learn about the interconnection of American and Australian history?

4. Prepare a summary of the main points of this article and discuss it with the class, especially the ethical questions.

Poems

Moreton Bay (c. 1840)

This anonymous ballad, also known as *The Convict's Lament*, is set in the penal[1] colony of Moreton Bay, near Brisbane, established in 1824 and run by its harsh commandant Captain Patrick Logan (1791–1830).

I am a native of the land of Erin[2],
And lately banished[3] from that lovely shore,
I left behind me my aged parents,
And the girl I adore.

In transit[4] storms as I set sailing,
Like a bold mariner[5] my coast did steer[6],
Sydney harbour was my destination –
That cursed[7] harbour at length drew near;
I then joined banquet[8] in congratulation
On my safe arrival from the briny[9] sea;
But alas[10]! alas! I was mistaken –
Twelve years transported to Moreton Bay.

Early one morning as I carelessly wandered,
By the Brisbane waters I chanced to stray[11],
I saw a prisoner sadly bewailing[12],
While on the sunbeaming banks he lay.
He said, I have been a prisoner at Port Macquarie[13]

---

[1] penal: having to do with punishment
[2] land of Erin (poetic): Ireland
[3] to banish: to force to leave as a punishment
[4] in transit: during the passage
[5] mariner (poetic): seaman
[6] to steer: to cause to move in a certain direction
[7] cursed ['kɜːsɪd]: *verflucht*
[8] banquet ['bæŋkwɪt]: formal meal with a large number of people
[9] briny ['braɪni]: containing a lot of salt
[10] alas (old-fashioned): *leider*
[11] to stray: to move away from the place where you should be
[12] to bewail: to express great sadness about s.th.
[13] Port Macquarie, etc.: were all settlements for convicts

At Norfolk Island, and Emu Plain,
At Castle Hill, and cursed Towngabbie –
And at all those places I've worked in chains;

But of all the places of condemnation
In each penal station of New South Wales
Moreton Bay I found no equal,
For excessive tyranny each day prevails[14].
Early in the morning, as the day is dawning,
To trace[15] from heaven the morning dew[16],
Up we are started at a moment's warning,
Our daily labour for to renew;

Our overseers and superintendents,
All these cursed tyrants' language we must obey,
Or else at the triangles[17] our flesh is mangled[18] –
That is our wages[19] at Moreton Bay.
For three long years I've been beastly treated;
Heavy irons each day I wore,
My poor back from flogging[20] has been lacerated[21],
And oftimes painted with crimson gore[22].

Like the Egyptians or ancient Hebrews,
We were sorely[23] oppressed by Logan's yoke[24],
Till kind Providence[25] came to our assistance,
And gave this tyrant his fatal stroke[26].

---

[14] to prevail: to be very common at a certain time
[15] to trace: (here): to make clearer
[16] dew [dju:]: *Tau*
[17] triangle: (here) three large and heavy sticks tied together at the top in which a convict is held and whipped
[18] to mangle: to twist and crush
[19] wages: *Lohn*
[20] to flog: to whip
[21] to lacerate: to cut skin or flesh with s.th. sharp
[22] crimson gore (fig.): thick blood from a wound
[23] sorely: very much
[24] yoke (fig.): *Joch*
[25] Providence: *die Vorsehung*
[26] stroke: act of hitting

Yes, he was hurried from that place of bondage[27],
Where he thought he would gain renown;
But a native black[28], who lay in ambush[29],
Gave this monster his fatal wound.

Now that I've got once more to cross the ocean,
And leave this place called Moreton Bay,
Where many a man from downright starvation[30]
Lies mouldering[31] to-day beneath the clay[32].
Fellow prisoners be exhilarated[33],
And your former sufferings don't bear in mind,
For it's when from bondage[34] you are extricated[35],
We will leave those tyrants far, behind.

1. Compare this poem with the short story, *How Muster-Master Stoneman Earned His Breakfast.*

---

[27] place of bondage: i.e. prison
[28] native black: Aborigine
[29] to lie in ambush: to wait in a hidden place from which to make a surprise attack – Patrick Logan is said to have been killed by an Aborigine by a blow to the head while exploring the land around Moreton Bay in the hope of becoming famous.
[30] downright starvation: a planned policy of not providing enough to eat
[31] to moulder: to slowly decay (*verwesen*)
[32] clay: (here): earth
[33] exhilarated: feeling happy and excited
[34] bondage (formal): state of being a prisoner
[35] to extricate (formal): (here): to free

The Song of Australia (1860)

by Caroline Carleton (1820–1874)

Caroline Carleton was born and educated in England. Her patriotic song won the first prize in a contest and was later set to music.

There is a land where summer skies
Are gleaming with a thousand dyes[36],
Blending in witching[37] harmonies;
And grassy knoll[38] and forest height
Are flushing[39] in the rosy light,
And all above is azure[40] bright –
Australia!

There is a land where honey flows,
Where laughing corn luxuriant grows,
Land of the myrtle[41] and the rose;
On hill and plain the clust'ring[42] vine[43]
Is gushing out[44] with purple wine,
And cups are quaffed[45] to thee and thine[46] –
Australia!

There is a land where treasures shine
Deep in the dark unfathom'd[47] mine
For worshippers at Mammon[48]'s shrine;
Where gold lies hid, and rubies gleam,

---

[36] dye: (here): colour
[37] witching: (here): *bezaubernd*
[38] knoll [nəʊl]: small, round hill
[39] to flush: to become red
[40] azure: bright blue
[41] myrtle: *Myrte*
[42] to cluster: (here): to grow closely together (in this case: the grapes)
[43] vine: *Weinrebe*
[44] to gush out: to flow suddenly and quickly
[45] to quaff (old-fashioned): to quickly drink a large quantity of s.th.
[46] thee and thine (old-fashioned): you and yours (singular)
[47] unfathomed: (here): not having been explored
[48] Mammon (biblical): riches, wealth as the only things important in life

And fabled wealth no more doth[49] seem
The idle[50] fancy[51] of a dream –
Australia!

There is a land where homesteads[52] peep[53]
From sunny plain and woodland steep,
And love and joy bright vigils keep[54];
Where the glad voice of childish glee[55]
Is mingling[56] with the melody
Of nature's hidden minstrelsy[57] –
Australia!

There is a land where floating free
From mountain top to girdling[58] sea
A proud flag waves exultingly!
And Freedom's sons the banner[59] bear[60],
No shackl'd[61] slave can breathe the air,
Fairest of Britain's daughters fair –
Australia!

1. What is meant by Mammon's shrine?

2. Compare this poem with the others.

3. Is this poem an example of good poetry?

4. How does this representation of Australia compare with the short stories?

---

[49] doth (old-fashioned): does
[50] idle: with no particular purpose
[51] fancy: s.th. imagined
[52] homestead: a piece of homeland given to you by the state
[53] to peep: to be just visible
[54] to keep vigil: to guard, to be watchful
[55] glee: feeling of happiness
[56] to mingle: to mix
[57] minstrelsy: like the singers of the Middle Ages
[58] to girdle (poetic): to surround
[59] banner: flag
[60] to bear: to carry
[61] shackled: in irons (i.e. metal rings around the ankles and wrists)

Waltzing Matilda[62] (1895)

by Banjo Paterson (1864–1941)

The words and song have become Australia's national song. Banjo Paterson often contributed to *The Bulletin.*

Oh! there once was a swagman[63] camped in the billabong[64],
Under the shade of a coolabah tree[65];
And he sang as he looked at his old billy[66] boiling,
"Who'll come a[67]-waltzing Matilda with me?"

Who'll come a-waltzing Matilda, my darling,
Who'll come a-waltzing Matilda with me?
Waltzing Matilda and leading a water-bag –
Who'll come a-waltzing Matilda with me?

Down came a jumbuck[68] to drink at the waterhole,
Up jumped the swagman and grabbed him in glee[69];
And he sang as he put him away in his tucker-bag[70],
"You'll come a-waltzing Matilda with me!"

Down came the squatter[71] a-riding his thoroughbred[72];
Down came policemen – one, two, and three.
Whose is the jumbuck you've got in the tucker-bag?
You'll come a-waltzing Matilda with me.'

---

62 to waltz Matilda (Australian English, informal): to travel the road with a bundle at the end of a stick (Matilda)
63 swagman (Australian English, informal): a man who travels around looking for work
64 billabong (Australian English): a waterhole
65 coolabah tree: Australian tree that produces a strong, hard wood
66 billy (Australian English): metal pot for boiling water
67 a- (old-fashioned): old English prefix that was used for verbs; similar to the German *ge-*
68 jumbuck (Australian English, informal): sheep
69 in glee: with a feeling of happiness
70 tucker-bag (Australian English, informal): bag for food
71 squatter (Australian English): a farmer with a large sheep farm or cattle ranch, often on land given to him by the British government
72 thoroughbred: horse of fine quality

But the swagman, he up and he jumped in the waterhole,
Drowning himself by the coolabah tree;
And his ghost may be heard as it sings in the billabong,
"Who'll come a-waltzing Matilda with me?"

1. Contrast this poem with *The Song of Australia.*

2. Why do you think this poem became so popular in Australia?

3. What other examples of class conflict can you find in the short stories?

Aboriginal Charter of Rights

by Oodgeroo of the Tribe Noonuccal (1920–1993), female Aboriginal poet, environmentalist and leader in the struggle for Aboriginal rights

We want hope, not racialism,
Brotherhood, not ostracism[73],
Black advance, not white ascendance[74]:
Make us equals, not dependants.
We need help, not exploitation,
We want freedom, not frustration;
Not control, but self-reliance,
Independence, not compliance[75],
Not rebuff[76], but education,
Self-respect, not resignation.
Free us from a mean subjection[77],
From a bureaucrat Protection.
Let's forget the old-time slavers[78]:

[73] ostracism: the act of deliberately not allowing s.o. to be included in a group
[74] ascendance: becoming politically and economically dominant
[75] compliance: the act of obeying rules or requests made by people in authority
[76] rebuff: being rejected
[77] subjection: being dominated
[78] slaver: person who sold or bought slaves

Give us fellowship, not favours;
Encouragement, not prohibitions,
Homes, not settlements and missions.
We need love, not overlordship,
Grip of hand, not whip-hand wardship[79];
Opportunity that places
White and black on equal basis.
You dishearten, not defend us,
Circumscribe[80], who should befriend us.
Give us welcome, not aversion,
Give us choice, not cold coercion[81],
Status, not discrimination,
Human rights, not segregation.
You the law, like Roman Pontius[82],
Make us proud, not colour-conscious;
Give the deal you still deny us,
Give goodwill, not bigot bias;
Give ambition, not prevention,
Confidence, not condescension[83];
Give incentive, not restriction,
Give us Christ, not crucifixion.
Though baptized[84] and blessed[85] and Bibled
We are still tabooed and libelled[86].
You devout[87] Salvation[88]-sellers,
Make us neighbours, not fringe-dwellers[89];
Make us mates, not poor relations,
Citizens, not serfs[90] on stations[91].

---

[79] wardship: guardianship, watching over a dependent person
[80] to circumscribe: to restrict
[81] coercion [kəʊˈɜːʃən]: the act of making s.o. do s.th. that they do not want to do with the possible use of force
[82] Roman Pontius: i.e., Pontius Pilate
[83] condescension: behaving in a way that shows you think you are superior to s.o. else
[84] to baptize: *taufen*
[85] to bless: *segnen*
[86] to libel [ˈlaɪbəl]: to publish a written statement about s.o. that is not true
[87] devout [dɪˈvaʊt]: *fromm*
[88] salvation (Christianity): the state of being saved from the power of evil
[89] fringe-dweller: person living at the edge of society
[90] serf: *Leibeigene(r)*
[91] station: (here): settlement for Aborigines

Must we native Old Australians
In our own land rank as aliens?
Banish[92] bans[93] and conquer caste,
Then we'll win our own at last.

1964

The Dispossessed

For Uncle Willie McKenzie

Peace was yours, Australian man, with tribal laws you made,
Till white Colonials stole your peace with rape[94] and murder raid[95];
They shot and poisoned and enslaved until, a scattered few,
Only a remnant now remain, and the heart dies in you.
The white man claimed your hunting grounds and you could not remain,
They made you work as menials[96] for greedy private gain[97];
Your tribes are broken vagrants[98] now wherever whites abide[99],
And justice of the white man means justice to you denied.
They brought you Bibles and disease, the liquor and the gun:
With Christian culture such as these the white command was won.
A dying race you linger on[100], degraded[101] and oppressed,
Outcasts in your own native land, you are the dispossessed.

When Churches mean a way of life, as Christians proudly claim,
And when hypocrisy[102] is scorned[103] and hate is counted shame,

---

92 to banish: to do away with s.th.
93 ban: prohibition
94 rape: *Vergewaltigung*
95 murder raid: a sudden surprise attack ending in murder
96 menial ['mi:niəl]: a person with a badly paid job requiring little skill
97 gain: profit
98 vagrant: a person who has no home or job and goes about begging
99 to abide (formal, old-fashioned): to reside, to live somewhere
100 to linger on: to continue to exist
101 degraded: treated in a way that shows no respect
102 hypocrisy [hɪˈpɒkrəsi]: *Scheinheiligkeit*
103 to scorn: *verachten*

Then only shall intolerance die and old injustice cease[104],
And white and dark as brothers find equality and peace.
But oh, so long the wait has been, so slow the justice due[105],
Courage decays[106] for want of[107] hope, and the heart dies in you.

1964

1. What is meant by "Salvation-sellers" and to "conquer caste"?
2. What government policies are being criticised in the poems?
3. Compare the issues dealt with in the poems with the short stories *Going Home* and *Marlene*.
4. What goals are expressed in the poems? How do you feel about them?
5. Compare "Make us neighbours, not fringe-dwellers" with the short story *Neighbours*.
6. Compare the poems with Martin Luther King's famous *I Have a Dream* speech.
7. What similarities can you find with the way the Native Americans of North America were treated by missionaries in the 16th, 17th, 18th, and 19th centuries?
8. What is the attitude towards Christianity in these poems?

[104] to cease [si:s] (formal): to no longer continue to exist
[105] due [dju:]: owed (*fällig*)
[106] to decay (fig.): to be gradually destroyed
[107] for want of: because of a lack of

Wednesday, 13 February 2008, House of Representatives Chamber

APOLOGY TO AUSTRALIA'S INDIGENOUS[1] PEOPLES

[...]
Mr Kevin Rudd[1] (Prime Minister)
(9.00 am)

I move[2]: That today we honour the Indigenous peoples of this land, the oldest continuing cultures in human history. We reflect on their past mistreatment. We reflect in particular on the mistreatment of those who were Stolen Generations – this blemished[3] chapter in our nation's history.

The time has now come for the nation to turn a new page in Australia's history by righting the wrongs of the past and so moving forward with confidence to the future. We apologise for the laws and policies of successive Parliaments and governments that have inflicted[4] profound grief, suffering and loss on these our fellow Australians.

We apologise especially for the removal of Aboriginal and Torres Strait Islander[5] children from their families, their communities and their country. For the pain, suffering and hurt of these Stolen Generations, their descendants and for their families left behind, we say sorry. To the mothers and the fathers, the brothers and the sisters, for the breaking up of families and communities, we say sorry. And for the indignity[6] and degradation[7] thus inflicted on a proud people and a proud culture, we say sorry.

---

1 Kevin Rudd: Kevin Rudd was forced to step down on 22 June 2010 and was replaced by his deputy, Julia Gillard, the nation's first female prime minister.
2 to move: to suggest formally
3 to blemish: to spoil s.th. that is otherwise perfect
4 to inflict: to make s.o. suffer s.th. unpleasant
5 Torres Straight Islanders: Aborigines living on the Torres Straight Islands that lie between the island of New Guinea and northern Australia
6 indignity: *Demütigung*
7 degradation: causing a loss of self-respect

We the Parliament of Australia respectfully request that this apology be received in the spirit in which it is offered as part of the healing of the nation. For the future we take heart; resolving[8] that this new page in the history of our great continent can now be written.

We today take this first step by acknowledging the past and laying claim to[9] a future that embraces[10] all Australians. A future where this Parliament resolves that the injustices of the past must never, never happen again. A future where we harness[11] the determination of all Australians, Indigenous and non-Indigenous, to close the gap[12] that lies between us in life expectancy, educational achievement and economic opportunity. A future where we embrace[13] the possibility of new solutions to enduring[14] problems where old approaches have failed. A future based on mutual respect, mutual resolve and mutual responsibility. A future where all Australians, whatever their origins, are truly equal partners, with equal opportunities and with an equal stake[15] in shaping the next chapter in the history of this great country, Australia.

Mr Speaker, there comes a time in the history of nations when their peoples must become fully reconciled to[16] their past if they are to go forward with confidence to embrace their future. Our nation, Australia, has reached such a time. That is why the Parliament is today here assembled: to deal with this unfinished business of the nation, to remove a great stain[17] from the nation's soul and, in a true spirit of reconciliation[18], to open a new chapter in the history of this great land, Australia.

Last year I made a commitment to the Australian people that if we formed the next government of the Commonwealth we would in Parliament say sorry to the Stolen Generations. Today I honour that commitment. I said we would do so early in the life of the new Parliament. Again, today I

8 to resolve: to make a firm decision
9 to lay claim to: to state that you have the right to own s.th.
10 to embrace: to include
11 to harness: to make use of s.th. to achieve s.th.
12 gap: *Lücke*
13 to embrace: (here): to accept s.th. with enthusiasm
14 enduring: lasting for a long time
15 stake: *Anteil*
16 reconciled ['rekənsaɪlɪd] to: accepting s.th. unpleasant
17 stain (fig.): mark that is difficult to remove
18 reconciliation: *Versöhnung*

honour that commitment by doing so at the commencement[19] of this the 42nd Parliament of the Commonwealth. Because the time has come, well and truly come, for all peoples of our great country, for all citizens of our great Commonwealth, for all Australians – those who are Indigenous and those who are not – to come together to reconcile and together build a new future for our nation.

Some have asked, "Why apologise?" Let me begin to answer by telling the Parliament just a little of one person's story – an elegant, eloquent and wonderful woman in her 80s, full of life, full of funny stories, despite what has happened in her life's journey, a woman who has travelled a long way to be with us today, a member of the Stolen Generation, who shared some of her story with me when I called around to see her just a few days ago. Nanna Nungala Fejo, as she prefers to be called, was born in the late 1920s. She remembers her earliest childhood days living with her family and her community in a bush camp just outside Tennant Creek[20]. She remembers the love and the warmth and the kinship[21] of those days long ago, including traditional dancing around the camp fire at night. She loved the dancing. She remembers once getting into strife[22] when, as a four-year old girl, she insisted on dancing with the male tribal elders rather than just sitting and watching the men, as the girls were supposed to do.

But then, sometime around 1932, when she was about four, she remembers the coming of the welfare men. Her family had feared that day and had dug holes in the creek[23] bank where the children could run and hide. What they had not expected was that the white welfare men did not come alone. They brought a truck, two white men and an Aboriginal stockman[24] on horseback cracking[25] his stock whip[26]. The kids were found; they ran for their mothers, screaming, but they could not get away. They were herded[27] and piled onto the back of the truck. Tears flowing, her mum

19 commencement (formal): beginning
20 Tennant Creek: town of 3,000 with a large Aboriginal population in the middle of the Northern Territory, also the scene of the 19th century Gold Rush
21 kinship: feeling of being in a family
22 strife: conflict
23 creek (Australian and American English): small river
24 stockman: man who is the owner of a large cattle ranch or sheep farm or works there
25 to crack: to make a sharp sound
26 stock whip: whip used for cattle
27 to herd (fig.): to force to move together

tried clinging[28] to the sides of the truck as her children were taken away to the Bungalow[29] in Alice[30], all in the name of protection.

A few years later, government policy changed. Now the children would be handed over to the missions to be cared for by the churches. But which church would care for them? The kids were simply told to line up in three lines. Nanna Fejo and her sisters stood in the middle line, her older brother and cousin on her left. Those on the left were told that they had become Catholics, those in the middle Methodists and those on the right Church of England. That is how the complex questions of post-reformation theology were resolved in the Australian outback in the 1930s. It was as crude[31] as that. She and her sister were sent to a Methodist mission on Goulburn Island[32] and then Croker Island[33]. Her Catholic brother was sent to work at a cattle station and her cousin to a Catholic mission. Nanna Fejo's family had been broken up for a second time. She stayed at the mission until after the war, when she was allowed to leave for a prearranged job as a domestic[34] in Darwin[35]. She was 16. Nanna Fejo never saw her mum again. After she left the mission, her brother let her know that her mum had died years before, a broken woman fretting for[36] the children that had literally[37] been ripped[38] away from her.

I asked Nanna Fejo what she would have me say today about her story. She thought for a few moments then said that what I should say today was that all mothers are important. And she added: "Families – keeping them together is very important. It's a good thing that you are surrounded by love and that love is passed down the generations. That's what gives you happiness." As I left, later on, Nanna Fejo took one of my staff aside, wanting to make sure that I was not too hard on the Aboriginal stockman who had hunted those kids down all those years ago. The stockman

28 to cling, clung, clung: to hold tightly
29 the Bungalow: a home for Aboriginal children
30 Alice: i.e. Alice Springs, second largest town in the Northern Territory
31 crude: simple and done without much care or thought
32 Goulburn Island: one of a group of small islands north of Australia's northern coast
33 Croker Island: another island off the coast of northern Australia
34 domestic: person working as a servant in s.o.'s home
35 Darwin: capital city of the Northern Territory on the northern coast of Australia
36 to fret for: to be worried about
37 literally: *wortwörtlich*
38 to rip: to pull with force

had found her again decades later, this time himself to say, "Sorry." And remarkably, extraordinarily, she had forgiven him.

Nanna Fejo's is just one story. There are thousands, tens of thousands, of them: stories of forced separation of Aboriginal and Torres Strait Islander children from their mums and dads over the better part of a century. [...]

The first 15 minutes are available as a video on You Tube:

http://www.youtube.com/watch?v=BljeWeDpc68

1. What universal truths are revealed in this speech?

2. What is your reaction to this speech?

3. Which of the short stories is most connected with this speech? Explain why.

4. Write a short story about Nanna Fejo's life.

5. Compare what you learn about the Stolen Generation with the two poems by Oodgeroo of the Tribe Noonuccal.

These days it's harder to be different

by Hsu-Ming Teo

[...]

Being Australian is more than formal citizenship; it is feeling like an Aussie as well. And it is harder today to be an Australian – an Aussie in a cultural, emotive[1], gut instinct[2] sort of way – than it was 10 years ago. A decade ago there were many ways of being Australian. Many proudly proclaimed that multiculturalism was one of the defining features of Australian identity.

Multiculturalism made ethnic Australians believe that mainstream society was interested in them and their experiences of being Australian. This was highlighted[3] in popular culture by such films as *Strictly Ballroom*[4] and *Heartbreak High*[5].

Multiculturalism was touted[6] as a political and cultural asset[7]. We were a model of a modern nation state with an ethnically and culturally diverse people who could live and work together. This was remarkable in a historical sense. With the exception of the United States, most countries have been forged[8] as modern nations on the basis of ethnic and cultural exclusivity. The history of the last century bears this out[9].

But Australia was different. Because of our appreciation[10] for diversity, we could act as a cultural mediator between East and West. It was an innately[11] arrogant assumption, but a happily optimistic one.

---

1 emotive: emotional
2 gut instinct: with purely emotional feelings
3 to highlight: to give special attention to s.th.
4 Strictly Ballroom: well-made 1992 Australian film about a ballroom dancer who refuses to accept the dancing of the establishment and takes on an "ugly-duckling" partner
5 Heartbreak High: The original film was later used as the basis for an Australian television series in the 1990s, dealing with the students of Hartley High, a tough high school in a multiracial area of Sydney.
6 to tout [taʊt]: to try to persuade people that s.th. is really good
7 asset: s.th. of value
8 to forge (fig.): to shape, to form
9 to bear out: to confirm (*bestätigen*)
10 appreciation: a full or sympathetic understanding of s.th.
11 innately: in essence

All this has changed. Australia may be a multicultural nation, but multiculturalism as a social and political ideal is under siege[12]. [...]

Once touted as the cure to racism, intolerance and assumptions about Anglo-Saxon cultural supremacy, multiculturalism is now cited as the cause of intolerance and racism.

A decade ago, multiculturalism defined a special and significant aspect of Australian national identity. Today it is regarded by some as incompatible with a national identity that is conceived[13] as unitary and homogeneous.

Yet nothing has arisen to replace the ideal of multiculturalism as a way of making Australians from different cultural backgrounds feel at home, to make them feel Australian. Instead, national identity has become narrowly and regressively[14] defined.

For a decade that identity has been publicly hauled[15] back to its conservative white male moorings[16]: Gallipoli and the Anzac legend, cricket, footy[17], mateship[18].

This may have given a sense of security to many, but it has also narrowed the ways in which one can be Australian. No wonder "un-Australian" is increasingly used as an epithet[19] of abuse[20].

The ideal of multiculturalism at least gave us all a chance to be equally Australian, in diverse and interesting ways.

Australian society dramatically changed its cultural and ethnic composition in the last quarter of the 20th century from predominantly Anglo-

---

12 under siege [siːdʒ]: under attack
13 to conceive: to consider
14 regressively: returning to an earlier stage of behaviour
15 to haul: to pull with a lot of effort
16 moorings (fig.): ropes and chains used to tie a ship or boat to a fixed place
17 footy (informal): football
18 mateship: for a discussion of Gallipoli, Anzac, and mateship consult the article, *Information About Australia*, p. 97
19 epithet [ˈepɪθet]: descriptive word or phrase
20 abuse: rude and offensive remark

European to multicultural. This was achieved remarkably peaceably, without overt[21] violence.

But it doesn't mean that the transition from White Australia to assimilation to integration and multiculturalism was without trauma. It would be difficult to imagine otherwise when there are Australians still living who fought in two world wars for many reasons, including a particular ideal of what their white community should be like.

For those Australians, it can't have been easy to see their neighbourhoods or swathes[22] of suburbs transformed. It is to their credit[23] that this occurred tranquilly[24] and relatively seamlessly[25].

Yet there still remains the problem of feeling "at home" in transformed neighbourhoods and communities, a problem that has not been sufficiently recognised or addressed; a problem which was suppressed and glossed over[26] with the insistence in the 1970s and 1980s that Australians are not racist but multicultural, until it found a lightning rod[27] in Pauline Hanson[28].

The popularity and success of Hanson was not surprising, not because Anglo-Australians are essentially racist but because a significant proportion of Australians had not been feeling "at home" in their own country for a long time but had not been able to articulate these views.

Ironically, this was shared by many migrants. The German word, "heimlich," in its original meaning in Middle High German, in the sense of "belonging to the house, not strange, but familiar, tame[29], intimate, friendly," is an excellent expression of this feeling.

---

[21] overt: done in the open, not secretly
[22] swathe [sweɪð]: large strip or area of s.th.
[23] to their credit: deserving of respect
[24] tranquilly: peacefully
[25] seamlessly: *nahtlos*
[26] to gloss over: to ignore a serious problem
[27] lightning rod: *Blitzableiter*
[28] Pauline Hanson (1954 –): Australian politician who supported a nationalist and anti-immigration policy – She now lives in Great Britain.
[29] tame: *zahm*

Ultimately, whether we believe in assimilation or multiculturalism, "heimlich" is what we all want. "Unheimlich," the opposite, means "concealed[30], kept from sight, so that others do not get to know about it". It's what happens when we like the food of those ethnics but know next to nothing about their lives.

Until now we've had Australians of all persuasions[31] not feeling at home, but unable to discuss it openly without the conversation being hijacked[32] into hysterical, hyperbolic accusations of racism or disloyalty to the nation. This has served to shut down dialogue and understanding.

The question is: does doing away with multiculturalism and opting for[33] a backward-looking, narrowly defined view of Australian culture serve to make more people feel at home in this nation?

Or will it simply reinforce[34] the instinctive idea that some people (white, English-speaking, Shire[35] Aussies) are naturally more Australian than others? What potential problems are created by alienating[36] and marginalising[37] people who find it hard to feel Australian in such a narrow way, which is ultimately based on culture, language, and even race?

[...] it would be wonderful if we could break the impasse[38], put away our sense of rights and entitlements[39], fears of racism or of being accused of racism, and sit down as individuals or community groups to talk to each other, to ask each other: what would it take, what can I do, to make you feel at home?

---

30 concealed: hidden
31 persuasion: set of beliefs or religion
32 to hijack: (here): to force
33 to opt for: to choose from several alternatives
34 to reinforce: to make s.th. stronger
35 Shire: i.e. "Sutherland Shire," which is a region south of Sydney where the Cronulla race riots of 2005 took place. The "Shire" is well-known for being very Anglo-Saxon, xenophobic and anti-immigrant. The leader of an insignificant white supremacist party has his base there.
36 to alienate: to make s.o. feel he/she doesn't belong to the group
37 to marginalise: to give s.o. a less important or lower position within a society or group
38 impasse: deadlock, situation which seems impossible to change
39 entitlement: (here): financial support given by the government to certain people

1. What parallels to the problems of multiculturalism in Australia can you find in your country, in Great Britain, the USA, France, and other countries with a large immigrant population?

2. Research the Cronulla race riots and other examples of racial violence in Australia that have occurred in the last two decades. Make a class presentation.

3. Which short stories does this article especially apply to? Explain.

The complete article originally appeared in *The Sydney Morning Herald,* December 7, 2006.

Edgar Allan Poe's[1] Definition of a Short Prose Narrative or Short Story

Were we called upon, however, to designate[2] that class of composition[3] which [...] should best fulfill the demands of high[4] genius – should offer it the most advantageous field of exertion[5] – we should unhesitatingly speak of the prose tale[6]. [...] We allude to[7] the short prose narrative, requiring[8] from a half-hour to one or two hours in its perusal[9]. The ordinary novel is objectionable[10], from its length, for reasons already stated in substance[11]. As it cannot be read at one sitting, it deprives itself [12], of course, of the immense force derivable[13] from totality. Worldly interests intervening[14] during the pauses of perusal, modify, annul[15] , or counteract, in a greater or less degree, the impressions of the book. But simple cessation[16] in reading, would, of itself, be sufficient to destroy the true unity. In the brief tale, however, the author is enabled to carry out the fullness of his intention, be it what it may. During the hour of perusal the soul of the reader is at the writer's control. There are no external or extrinsic[17] influences – resulting from weariness[18] or interruption.

---

1 Edgar Allan Poe [pəʊ]: (1809–1849): American writer and critic – This extract is from Poe's 1842 criticism of the American writer Nathaniel Hawthorne's (1804–1864) short story anthology, **Twice Told Tales**.

2 to designate: to select

3 composition: writing

4 high: great

5 field of exertion: means of achieving the best creative writing

6 prose tale: story written in prose, not poetry (prose = Prosa)

7 to allude to s.th.: (here): to refer to

8 to require: to need

9 in its perusal (formal): to read it

10 objectionable: causing a feeling of dislike or opposition

11 in substance: (here): with specific examples

12 to deprive oneself/itself of s.th.: to prevent oneself/itself from having or enjoying s.th.

13 derivable: coming

14 to intervene: to interfere

15 to annul [əˈnʌl]: to remove, to cancel

16 cessation in reading (formal): no longer continuing to read

17 extrinsic: coming from outside instead of inside

18 weariness: being tired

A skilful[19] literary artist has constructed a tale. If wise, he has not fashioned[20] his thoughts to accommodate[21] his incidents; but having conceived[22], with deliberate[23] care, a certain unique or single effect to be wrought out[24], he then invents such incidents – he then combines such events as may best aid him in establishing this preconceived[25] effect. If his very initial[26] sentence tend not[27] to the out-bringing of this effect, then he has failed in his first step. In the whole composition there should be no word written, of which the tendency, direct or indirect, is not to the one pre-established design. And by such means, with such care and skill, a picture is at length painted which leaves in the mind of him who contemplates[28] it with a kindred[29] art,[30] a sense of the fullest satisfaction.

1. Why does Poe prefer the short story to the novel? Do you agree? Explain.

2. Comment on his style.

3. To what extent do the five short stories correspond to Edgar Allan Poe's definition of a short story?

---

19 skilful: able to do s.th. well
20 to fashion: (here): to form
21 to accommodate: to fit with
22 to conceive: to work out a thought or idea
23 deliberate: carefully planned
24 wrought [rɔ:t] out (formal, past or past participle only): formed, fashioned
25 preconceived: worked out, planned in advance
26 initial [ɪˈnɪʃəl]: first
27 tend not (old-fashioned): doesn't tend to
28 to contemplate s.th.: to look at s.th. in a careful way for a long time
29 kindred [ˈkɪndrəd]: similar
30 art: (here): feelings and reactions that were intended by the author

Suggestions for Further Reading

The Literature of Australia, Nicholas Jose, editor, Norton, New York, 2009
useful anthology from the 18th century to the present

Die Aborigines Australiens, Gerhard Leitner, Verlag C. H. Beck, Munich, 2006

The Best Australian Short Stories, Mary Lord, editor, Penguin Books, Ringwood, Victoria, Australia, 1991

Australian Literature, Elizabeth Webby, editor, Cambridge University Press, Cambridge, 2000

The Slap, Christos Tsiolkas, Penguin, New York, 2010
novel about Greek immigrants to Australia

Blueback, Tim Winton, Picador, London, 1997
fable-like novel about the misuse of the oceans

Tales of the Convict System, Price Warung, The Bulletin, Sydney, 1892

Going Home, Stories by Archie Weller, Allen & Unwin, Crows Nest, NSW, Australia, 1986

Sorry, Gail Jones, Vintage Books, London, 2008
novel about the friendship between a white and Aboriginal girl

Australia, Susan Bambrick, Cambridge University Press, Cambridge, 1994
geography and history of Australia

The Oxford Literary History of Australia, Bruce Bennett, Jennifer Strauss, editors, Oxford University Press, Oxford, 1998

Australian Short Fiction, Bruce Bennett, University of Queensland Press, St. Luca, Queensland, Australia, 2002

Encyclopedia of Post-Colonial Literatures in English, Eugene Benson, editor, Volumes 1 and 2, Routledge, London, 1994

Visibly Different, Face, Place and Race in Australia, Maureen Perkins, editor, Peter Lang, Bern 2007

The Penguin New Literary History of Australia, Bruce Bennett et al., editor, Penguin, Ringwood, Victoria, Australia, 1988

A Concise History of Australia, Stuart Macintyre, Cambridge University Press, Cambridge, 2004

"Black Magic," nationalism and race in Australian football, David McNeill, pp. 22–37 in **Race & Class**, Volume 49, April – June 2008, Number 4

Being black in Australia: a case study of intergroup relations, Val Colic-Peisker and Farida Tilbury, pp. 38 – 55 in **Race & Class**, Volume 49, April – June 2008, Number 4

Henry Lawson, A. A. Phillips, Twayne Publishers, New York, 1970

Happiness, Selected Short Stories by Katharine Susannah Prichard, Angus and Robertson, Sydney, 1967

Henry Lawson, Selected Stories, HarperCollins, Sydney, 2001

Scission, Tim Winton, Penguin, Ringwood, Victoria, Australia, 1985
collection of short stories

The Fatal Shore, Robert Hughes, Vintage, London, 2003, first published in 1986
well-written and entertaining history of the transportation of convicts to Australia

Love and Vertigo, Hsu-Ming Teo, Allen & Unwin, Crows Nest, NSW, Australia, 2000
immigrant novel

Films About Australia

Australia (2007)
Though a long-drawn-out soap opera, it reveals much of the Australian mentality and the problem of The Stolen Generation.

Rabbit-Proof Fence (2002)
excellent film that deals with the problem of The Stolen Generation

Crocodile Dundee (1986)
entertaining comedy in spite of the clichés
Watch out for examples of mateship, clash of cultures, and the sympathetic treatment of Aborigines (who speak better English than the Aussies).

Strictly Ballroom (1992)
anti-establishment film about ballroom dancing

Heartbreak High
film and then Australian television series in the 1990s, dealing with the students of Hartley High, a fictitious, tough high school in a multiracial area of Sydney – available as a DVD

Gallipoli (1981)
The first hour of the film gives a wonderful snapshot of life in the outback in 1915.

The Man from Snowy River (1982) Australian film about manhood, based on the poem of the same name by Banjo Paterson

Some Useful Literary Terms

Allegory: a narrative in verse or prose in which specific characters and actions represent abstract ideas or moral qualities – An allegory can be literal, or real, and have symbolic levels of meaning.

Alliteration: the repetition of consonant or vowel sounds at the beginning of words

Allusion: a reference to a person, place, event, or written work such as the Bible that the author expects the reader to recognise

Anaphora: the repetition of the same word or words at the beginning of successive phrases, clauses, or sentences

Antagonist: the character or force that opposes the protagonist or hero in a conflict

Archaism: a word or expression that is out of date

Argumentation: writing or a speech that tries to convince the reader of the logic and merits of a particular viewpoint by giving specific reasons and examples

Characterisation: the means used by the author to develop the character, e.g. by description, what the character thinks or says, how he/she reacts or speaks, and how the other characters react or describe the character; the character may be superficially described or flat, or made to seem very real and complex: round.

Climax: the turning point of the story, the crisis, after which there seems to be no other possible way for the plot to continue – The part of the plot before the climax is often called **rising action** and that after the climax **falling action.**

Commentary: The author inserts his or her own comments or views.

Complication: the point in the story at which the conflict is introduced, thus giving the plot a new impetus

Conflict: the clash between opposing forces – It can involve ideas, persons, the forces of nature and be in the mind or external.

Dénouement: the part of a story or play when all questions are answered, secrets are revealed, conflicts are resolved, also called **resolution** or **outcome**

Description: The author tries to give the reader a mental image of what can be seen, felt, or heard by giving concrete descriptions, often to create a certain atmosphere.

Dialogue: what the characters actually say

Diction: the choice of words used by the author to produce a certain effect on the reader

Doppelgänger: a duplicate of a character, often of a mysterious or ghostly nature

Dramatic Irony: when a character says something without realising the true significance of what was said, however, it is obvious to the reader

Euphemism: the substitution of a mild or less negative word or phrase for a direct one, as in the use of "to pass away" instead of "to die"

Exposition: the part of a story, usually at the beginning, that gives essential background information for an understanding of the unfolding plot

Farce: comedy, usually about something ridiculous, often with stock characters

Fairy Tale: magical story for children (*Märchen*)

Flashback: a scene in a story or play that interrupts the action to show what happened in the past

Foil: character who is the opposite of another character in order to point up the strengths or weaknesses of the other character

Foreshadowing: a hint that something, usually bad, is going to happen later

Frame Story: a story with a framework, for example a narrator who, from a later point of time, describes what happened in the past, or a story within a story

Hyperbole: an exaggeration

Imagery: vivid sensory details that arouse certain emotions or feelings in the reader

Irony: when the author or a character means the opposite of what he/she actually writes or says

Metaphor: a direct comparison between two apparently different things, ideas, or persons without using *as* or *like*, i.e. She had rose lips.

Motivation: the force that drives a character to take a certain course of action

Mood: overall atmosphere of a work

The Other: a concept that has its origin in psychology – It describes the tendency of a dominant group to look upon different cultural or religious groups as strange and different, even inferior. For example, British colonisers often considered indigenous people under their control, in Africa, India, Australia, or New Zealand, as barbarous and uncivilised, who needed to be brought to the level of Western education and morals. **Othering** is the process of putting the stamp of **the other** on a person or persons.

Oxymoron: the combining of two terms that contradict each other, e.g. a cold fire

Paradox: a statement that seems to be contradictory

Personification: giving human or even animal qualities to objects or things

Plot: the plan and arrangement of related incidents within a story

Point of View: the manner in which the author presents the events and characters in a story

1. first-person narrator: The story is told by a character in the story, the "I" in the story.
2. limited third-person narrator who focuses on one character
3. omniscient third-person or an all-knowing observer who can describe and comment about everything and everyone in the story

Polysydeton: a rhetorical device whereby a conjunction, often *and*, is used repeatedly – frequently used in the Bible

Protagonist: the main character in a story on whom the action centres

Register: the kind of language used in a specific social setting – Examples of register are slang, colloquial, and formal. The kind of register used often reflects the social status of the character or may be purposely used in the wrong context or setting.

Repetition: repeating a word or phrase in a sentence to produce an effect

Sarcasm: the use of ironic remarks to show you dislike s.o.

Satire: the use of sarcasm or irony to show the moral weakness of people, an idea, a movement, a country, etc.

Setting: the physical background of a story, place and time

Simile: a direct comparison between two basically different things, ideas, or persons using *as* or *like*, i.e. She had lips like a rose.

Stock Character or Stereotype: a character with typical characteristics who keeps reappearing in literature, such as the jealous husband, the all-knowing but silent butler, the absent-minded professor, the hypocritical preacher

Stream of Consciousness: often considered the same as **interior monologue** – the thoughts and impressions of a character which are set down just as they occur in his/her mind

Suspense: the feeling of uncertainty and anxiety as the plot rises towards its climax

Symbol: anything that has a meaning in itself, but also stands for something larger than itself

Topos, plural **Topoi:** a traditional theme or motif, such as the jealous husband, young lovers, good overcoming evil, the servant of several masters (picaroon) who is able to trick them all, the beautiful woman who bewitches all men, the mad scientist, the devil buying souls

Picture references:

Page 7: www.adb.online.anu.edu.au
Page 26: Wikimedia Commons / Lawson Private Collection
Page 41: Katharine Susannah Prichard Writers Centre / Karen Throssel
Page 59: © Allen & Unwin, Sidney, Australia
Page 81: © Leon Bird, Perth, Australia
Page 90/91: Dipl.-Ing. Joachim Zwick, Gießen